The Word in Small Boats

THE WORD IN SMALL BOATS

Sermons from Oxford

Oliver O'Donovan

Edited by Andy Draycott

WILLIAM B. EERDMANS PUBLISHING COMPANY

GRAND RAPIDS, MICHIGAN / CAMBRIDGE, U.K.

Published 2010 by

Wm. B. Eerdmans Publishing Co.

2140 Oak Industrial Drive N.E., Grand Rapids, Michigan 49505 /

P.O. Box 163, Cambridge CB3 9PU U.K.

Printed in the United States of America

15 14 13 12 11 10   7 6 5 4 3 2 1

Library of Congress Cataloging-in-Publication Data

O'Donovan, Oliver.

   The word in small boats: sermons from Oxford / Oliver O'Donovan.

      p.   cm.

   ISBN 978-0-8028-6453-6 (pbk.: alk. paper)

   1. Sermons, English — 20th century.

   2. Sermons, English — 21st century.

   I. Title.

BV4253.O36   2010

252.00942 — dc22

                                      2009043729

www.eerdmans.com

Contents

Editor's Foreword

Oliver O'Donovan's preaching ministry as an ordained Anglican priest predates by some years the material surveyed for this collection. Oliver speaks particularly warmly of the congregation of Little Trinity Church, Toronto, whose patient and gifted listening blessed some of his formative early preaching. The sermons set out here, gathered from a store covering nearly a quarter of a century, are from that ministry taken up on his return from Canada to England. His job in Oxford was both a University and a Church appointment: as Regius Professor of Moral and Pastoral Theology and Canon of Christ Church Cathedral, respectively. He was appointed happily to teach and to preach.

Most of the sermons gathered here were preached in Christ Church. The first exception is the introductory sermon, "A Word Travelling in Small Boats", lending itself eponymously to the collection as a whole. It is in a sense a theological statement about, and celebration of, preaching and the preacher. There is one Word but there are many preachers, subject to disciplines of *that* ministry, amongst the manifold ministries of the church. This sermon opens the reader up to the glory and humility, the joy of the ministry of the word that Oliver finds in both its inward and outward directions. As one bookend to the collection it stands opposite another sermon from Acts as the concluding chapter. It could hardly be otherwise. "No End to the Word" was Oliver's valedictory sermon at Christ Church upon his move from Oxford to Edinburgh. We might say that this is the most self-conscious of the sermons, looking back, as it does, over that Oxford ministry as a whole to which he had been called.

The symmetry of opening and closing the collection with sermons from the book of Acts should not be lost on the reader attentive to their missionary bent. We may recognise, with Oliver, that last assigned lectionary reading as a providential gift in the distribution of Cathedral duties. Reflecting on his ministry as Canon Professor, Oliver underlines the boldness both of speech and of hearing that comprises the tri-polar communication of the word of God, "involving speaker, hearer, and the Spirit of God with both".

It is important to take note of the liturgical setting of the cathedral. It is clearly reflected in the Ascension sermon on the *Te Deum,* "The Opening of the Kingdom", as well as "The Sea! The Sea!" which takes up the verse of Psalm 95 from the liturgy of the word for Matins. The varying length of the sermons corresponds to the particular form of the service and reflects Oliver's discipline of speaking from a prepared full script. Which is to say that, allowing for any unscripted aside, the sermons here presented are the sermons as spoken. This accounts also for the form of writing, which is intended first to be heard rather than read, and no adjustments have been made to change this for this setting. Similarly, the conventions of spoken English reflect their cultural setting, and variations, such as there are, reflect the passage of time and a critical appropriation of some contemporary concerns.

The word preached locates the church in the here and now of her particular mission. Just so, the sermons have their local flavour, a flavour that, far from making them unpalatable to the far-flung reader long after their delivery, seasons the ongoing grappling with Scripture in mission for Christ's glory that is the daily bread of all his disciples. Therefore, we learn something of Christ Church's congregational setting and its personalities. Indeed, we should worry if we did not. It is an ancient university community, wherein a preponderantly older body of worshippers gather, happier, perhaps, with the fine points of intellectual striving and not given to spontaneous vocal response. But, most importantly, their habits of hearing scripture are formed by the lectionary, and it is to the exigencies of this order that most of the sermons are obedient. So much so that Oliver offers an apology when he strays, albeit couched in the confident exercise of evangelical liberty, in "Dividing the Kingdom". All the sermons, nevertheless, take their authority and authorisation from scripture.

Editor's Foreword

It is in service of God's word that sermons are delivered. A collection aims to demonstrate what this particular vocation to preaching has looked like. An effort has been made to ensure some sort of representation to the span of years covered, the genre of biblical text preached from, and — a more subjective judgment — the *kinds* of sermon. This judgment of kind is what has led to the collection being set out in four main parts. All this is framed by the conviction, born, in equal measure, from reading his books as well as his sermons, that mission is the governing *motif* of Oliver's thought.

So, pairing the first two sections, the *mission* of God's word comes before the *community* of God's word. This ordering serves as a deliberate caution to the ecclesiological creep in recent theology, whilst firmly affirming the importance of the church in mission. The second pair of sections is, in a sense, more interchangeable. Oliver's focused scholarly concentration on political theology over the last two decades means that readers familiar with that work will want to see both the seeds and the fruit of that labour in sermon form. It is to avoid the impression that this is the pinnacle of Christian reflection to which all preachers must aspire that "Tradition, Truth, and the Public" is not placed, climatically, last. "Launched upon Life by God's Word" takes up broader concerns of Christian life in the world.

The task of selection has been guided by a desire to allow the sermons to mirror the scope of Oliver's theological writings. Yet this aim should not be misconstrued. This is not a collection of *political* sermons, say, or sermons *on ethics,* although both forms of practical reason must appear. Theology cannot subscribe to such compartmentalisation, and certainly no call to preaching requisitioned by God's word could manage such a precise concentration to the exclusion of all else. Of course, if the collection serves to underline Oliver's missiological emphasis discerned elsewhere, well and good. It will do so most precisely as attention is focused on Jesus Christ. Which is to say that whilst the address of a sermon often assumes a more personal form than theological writing, offering the reader a perspective on the life-situation and thought-patterns of the preacher, it is not the aim of the sermons to stand in for biography. Certainly we cannot miss, for example, Oliver's love of Bach, his pointing to his own roots in the pietist tradition of the British evangelical Anglican world, and his ecumenical concerns. Yet a different selection would have been made were the aim to maximise that kind of biographical montage.

We proceed to outline the contents of each section in further detail, noting that a collection of sermons is precisely that. It is not a series of episodes telling a tightly defined story or expounding, verse by verse, a portion of scripture as if it were an applied commentary. Each sermon is a discrete sermon, not composed sequentially, following one on the other. Rather, they are spoken as the Holy Spirit gives discernment of the prophetic need of each particular occasion. A ministry of one Word inevitably allows themes to recur, just as sermons placed in one section might easily fit another.

"The Mission of God's Word" focuses our attention on the shape of the gospel. It is the concrete shape of the Christ event that determines all else. We open with an advent sermon, "A New Message", expounding the place of prophecy to the nations out of the history of Israel, whose God is coming. Two epiphany sermons are followed by preaching that takes up Jesus' ministry and passion, resurrection and return, ascension and Pentecost, and the Trinity. The double epiphany points to the bold dynamite of God's gospel initiative in Christ and the invitation to evangelism, in conjunction with the task of recognition. By warm illustration, "The Witness" takes us to John the Baptist and the question of his and our recognition of Jesus. For us this recognition can only be by the authority of scripture. Sight, once given, summons and completes faith, empowering witness. This relation of faith and sight runs through several sermons. "Travelling to Jerusalem" takes up the theme of journeying. Jesus' journey to Jerusalem intends a meeting, the hopeful travel of mission, open to encounter that is shaped by that ultimate goal. Jesus' journey defines our journey, as the pattern to which we are conformed, pointing us to the judgment made in meetings as the judgment we find in encounter with the Christ. As Christ, "The Servant", is our authoritative representative, according to Isaiah 53, then the political act of responsible speech is given to us. "Seeing the Risen One" again takes up the faith and sight relation, in setting out the passivity of our seeing the resurrection which still awaits its completion in Jesus' eschatological coming. "The Opening of the Kingdom" explores the creed exegetically, asking what it means that the kingdom of heaven is opened to all believers by him who will come to be our judge. Finally, in the Pentecost sermon, "Eternal Fire", we hear that the new and eternal can, truly, be reconciled, as the Spirit recapitulates Christ for and to us, enabling our newness of action.

Section two addresses the church as "The Community of God's Word". The first sermon, "Come!", harking back to the empowerment of Pentecost, examines the churchly task of prayer. It also offers encouragement to those who undertake the task of sermon-writing. "Left Behind in the Place", preached for a bishop's inauguration, is less an exposition or apology for ecclesiastical institutions of ministry than a missionary account of the place and living tradition of the church by the power of the Spirit. "Dividing the Kingdom" and "Asking" locate the congregation in the life and health of the Anglican church, worldwide and then nationally. Sex and money provide the backdrops respectively. The former addresses the threat of schism by warning the church that its freedom is curtailed as church if it is tempted to dwell on itself as the path to unity. The latter, a Rogation Sunday sermon from Luke 11:9, enjoins the, at least to the English, embarrassing command to ask. So we hear of prayer about little, vast, and, most difficult of all, local things where action falls into our area of responsibility. Between these two the importance of reading is commended from the church to the University around it. "Coming to Mount Zion" meditates on the meaning of perfection as we observe the imperfections of our own and other lives. "Frideswide's Place" anchors the church locally with the history given in place, looking to Christ Church's twelfth-century beginnings as a monastery at the site of a shrine to the still earlier St. Frideswide.

Section three, "Tradition, Truth, and the Public", begins with a sermon on the book of Daniel that opens out the clear perspective that governs the thread of the whole section. Mercifully, the horror felt before the sheer enormity and chaos of life's flow of events is narratable as God's history by the divine word of truth. This coherence and meaningfulness are what allow the church to recognise the truth of the gospel as the truth of the world, sustained through tradition in the public sphere. This is the movement of the section from Horror to Hallelujah. There follows a chronologically ordered series of sermons that place the church in the world of turmoil, from the fall of the Berlin Wall, through conflicts in Iraq and Kosovo, to terrorist attacks and their commemoration. These breakdowns in civility contrast with the claims of

Western democratic society for the virtuous practice of elections. The relative "Glory" of election campaigns and public office must be framed in the light of Jesus Christ. These sermons clearly show preaching as public speech that may form collective deliberation on and for the common good. In closing the section, further light is shed on the importance of Revelation for a Christian reading of contemporary public life in Oliver's thought. The last word of this section is then of "Hallelujah!" On the verge of the second Iraq war, it sets Spirit-empowered human praise in the context of God's victorious rule, and in this way appropriately locates penultimate judgments, even those of war and the threat of war. This is the gospel praise of "Hallelujah" that has replaced the fainting terror that overcame the prophet Daniel.

"Launched upon Life by God's Word" takes its title from the maritime treatment of Psalm 95:5 in "The Sea! The Sea!" The occasion for this sermon on the liturgy rather than the lectionary was determined by the unusual presence of a maritime conference in the college at the time. Again we take up the journeying metaphor destined towards home that is with God. If the buffeting waves of life are to teach us how to live, we need look to God for wisdom. The second sermon of this section Oliver entitles "How to Be a Human Being". It is followed by a sermon addressing that never-so-private-as-we-would-suppose phenomenon of wealth and possessions. "Possessing Wisdom" addresses more directly the University setting of Christ Church, asking whether the University might hope to impart true wisdom. The sermon on "The Honour of Marriage" echoes the maritime metaphor that frames the section, exploring the storm-battered relationship of the family in society, casting marriage as a ship borne aloft on the tempestuous waters of life. Finally come two sermons looking at the individual self from another angle. From Philippians 3:13 Oliver addresses the transition from flesh to spirit, setting out, at one point, an application to those of advancing years. Job 38:1 on "Facing Death" addresses the reality of death, in the lived life of the Cathedral congregation, and in joyful wonder before God.

Of omissions or simple absences we note that in a Cathedral it is the bishop who preaches on the feasts of Christmas and Easter. Preaching in the context of a baptism, for example, has not made it in, nor have any from Remembrance Sunday. Reading many more sermons than could

Editor's Foreword

appear here has been a blessing. Oliver's willingness to meet and discuss, improve and revise the ongoing selection of his sermons as the collection took shape has revealed the extent of his joy in this aspect of his ministry. None of this would have been possible without his cooperation and active encouragement.

ANDY DRAYCOTT
Aberdeen

Introduction: A Word Travelling in Small Boats

We tore ourselves away from them and,
putting to sea, made a straight run.   ACTS 21:1

A nice dramatic translation, that, from The Revised English Bible, cap-turing the intensity of Paul's farewell to the elders of the church at Ephesus: "We tore ourselves away". And there is more "tearing away" to come. St. Paul's company puts in at Tyre; the disciples there urge him to give up his journey; but a week later they have to escort him to the beach, kneel down and pray with him, and bid goodbye. In Ptolemais there is just a single day spent with the brotherhood. In Caesarea "all the local people", we are told, "beg and implore" the apostle to stay put, but once again he hits the road, escorted on his way by local Christians. As we follow Paul on these last steps of his journey round the Eastern Mediter-ranean, we meet at each place the same tension: the local community wants to keep him with them, he presses on determinedly to Jerusalem.

What is it that draws Paul forward towards the conflict that faces him? What is it that makes the churches want to hold him back? There is a personal element in it, of course. They care for his safety, and he cares for the responsibility he bears, which is to give the apostolic church an account of all that God has done among the Gentiles. But underneath the personal urgency there is a universal urgency, which lies at the heart of the church's existence: the urgency of the word of God itself.

25th September 2005, at St. Mary's Islington.

What makes the church? We have a simple description early in the Acts of the Apostles: *They devoted themselves to the apostles' teaching and to fellowship, to the breaking of bread and to prayers* (2:42). On the one hand the apostles' teaching, on the other, fellowship, material and spiritual. On the one hand the universal word of the apostolic gospel, on the other the local gathering of believers who share meals and pray together. On the one hand something common to all believers in all times and places, on the other something particular to one time and place. From the beginning the church is universal and local, catholic and particular, spread throughout the world and gathered, one and many.

And as we read on in the Acts of the Apostles we find this reflected in a *twofold service* that supports the church. There is the service of the word, on the one hand; there is the service of "tables", on the other. A useful word, "tables". In the ancient world you served food on them and you used them to count money on. All material and pastoral administration is summed up in the service of tables. And out of this twofold service there developed the ministries we now know as bishops, priests, and deacons. Three forms of ministry; but the essential point is that the service God equips the church for is twofold: turned inward, and turned outward. There is the intensive care of the gathering community; there is the extensive outreach of missionary communication. The inward horizon of charity links us in neighbourhood and mutual service; the outward horizon of proclamation reaches to the ends of the earth.

Paul is carried forward by the ministry of the word. The word is universal, and never allows him to put down roots. *The word of God is not bound,* as he wrote when he found himself for a short spell incommodiously restricted by four prison walls, but got through them by sending one of his precious letters. As the word of life was always moving — out from Jerusalem where the news of Christ began, round the known world, and back again to Jerusalem — so its minister was on the move. And the word and its minister left behind them a chain of local communities, each giving concrete and enduring witness *in its one place* to the power of the gospel to give life *in all places.* When Paul set out on this journey, we were told (Acts 18:23), he went to *settle* all the disciples. He has taken in Ephesus, Corinth, Philippi, Troas, Miletus, Ptolemais, Tyre, Caesarea on his way, and in each place there is a settled community of love and worship and praise.

It is the idols of whom the Psalmist says that *they have mouths but speak not, and they do not make a sound in their throat* (Ps. 115:5, 7). Of the living God, on the other hand, we read that *his word runs very swiftly* (Ps. 147:15). It goes forth from Jerusalem still, the place of God's self-disclosure on earth, and the gate by which it issues is that of Holy Scripture, the testimony of apostles and prophets who saw with their eyes and touched with their hands God come among us in Jerusalem. And the Word still circles the earth and returns to where it came from, bringing God back the praise he covets, the true tale of what he has done. *So it is with the word that goes forth from my mouth, it will not return to me empty* (Isa. 55:11). And, as on that journey of Paul's, the word of the Lord heads unflinchingly towards its moment of conflict, ready to do battle with the lies that vex God's ransomed earth. For the only possible point of reconciliation is the message of life, and the message of death must be banished. If this sounds very imperialistic, we must understand that the mission of this word is God's, not ours. It is not a mission to propagate our household arrangements and systems, nor to impose our local perspectives on whatever ground we happen to set our feet. It is to cast the gospel abroad as a seed that will bear its fruit wherever it grows. The Word is the possession of each community that receives it; its authority is shared by all to whom it has given life.

That is why Christians in the West are bound to listen to the voices of the Asian and African churches that speak to us about our common life as Christians. Next month will see the very important conference of the Anglican churches of the global South meeting in Egypt on the theme of "one holy, catholic and apostolic church". It is not that their word on any question has to be the last word. It is simply that we shall never know what the last word is unless we have first attended to their word, weighed it up and learned from it. Historically, our Northern churches were in place before most, though not all, of theirs. That does not entitle us to treat them as less than full partners. I won't say what I think of a certain mission society that has been putting around a poster bearing the words "Meet the World Church", and showing a picture of a grinning Asian peasant clutching a live chicken in his arms. That kind of patronising image stops us learning from churches with extensive experience of the perils and opportunities of globalised modernity and a high sophistication in thinking about it. The word has borne fruit among them, a testimony of praise that we — we, above all — may not ignore.

What vessels of transport does the word employ as it makes its sweeping voyage from one end of the world to the other? Not the mighty multi-volume encyclopedias that ply the grand cruise-lines from library to library. The word travels in small boats, the thought and speech of human beings, living the life of faith like any other believer but set aside for this ministry. Few vessels are less capacious than the mind of a single person, and so the word requisitions many of them rather than relying on one or two big preachers. Once requisitioned, they are subject to an austere discipline to fit them out: a discipline of living constantly with, and out of, the text of Holy Scripture; a discipline of bending the mind to the question, of focussing the point of intersection where Scripture sheds its light upon our living concerns; a discipline of patient dialectic and argument, teasing out each aspect of a question carefully and justly, for difficulties lying unresolved in the hold will make the boat list and divert it from its straight course; a discipline of studying the journeys Christian preachers have made before them, learning of shoals and currents; a discipline of speech, carefully clothing the Word with our words, not saying the first thing that comes into our head, riding the dangerous current of rhetorical fashion or polite observation, but searching and wrestling to find the apt word, the fitting word, the word that glorifies and adorns the Word of God itself.

To be requisitioned for the service of the word of God is to be committed to this perpetual and incessant voyage. One may sit at the same desk in the same room for forty years, the very image of sedentary and unadventurous stability, and yet be caught up in the *perpetuum mobile* of the word. New questions, new problems, new discoveries. And new dangers! Pray for your ministers of the word, that they may not lose their way upon the trackless ocean. When the Scriptures slip from their hands and their thoughts run free upon their own preoccupations, they are in danger. When they shy from the bitter moment of confrontation with lies and deception, they are in danger. But equally, when they become locked into postures of conflict as though a muscle somewhere in the mind had seized up, unable to follow the word's agile course through to the point of truth which will reconcile, then they are in danger. When their minds develop their own habits and they say the same things week after week, turning round in circles instead of making a straight run, then they are in danger upon the high seas.

Today Graham Kings, your Vicar, marks five years of ministering the word here and twenty-five years of ordained ministry. What shall we say upon this pleasant occasion? Perhaps you will say, "How well he has settled down! A real Islingtonian!" I would rather you said, *The word of God is not bound!* Graham's ministry was a gift to Islington from Kenya and from Cambridge. One day he will be a gift from Islington to somewhere else. The stay may be long, it may be short. The main thing is, it must not cease to be, even while he sits here in the Vicarage, a journey round the world. The whole Scriptures, the whole apostolic doctrine, the whole Christian life, the whole world church must break in on Islington through his ministry.

St. Mary's Islington has a long and distinguished history of service to the gospel. Before my only previous visit, I had known about its leading role in the eighteenth-century evangelical revival. Then thirty-eight years ago, when I was a student, I came here on the annual Islington week for those exploring a vocation to the ministry. There was at that time, as I recall, a curate in his first year of ministry, so astonishingly youthful in appearance that you might have thought he was ordained straight out of his pram. Though I never spoke personally with him, his account of his early experiences of ministry had a freshness about it that had a curious effect on me. "If this baby-face can cope with it, I expect even I can," I thought. Today he is a revered greybeard theologian on the other side of the globe. Islington's contribution, then as always, bore its fruit far beyond the roar of London's traffic. But well-settled churches face a standing temptation: to settle back into themselves, to draw entirely on their own experience and history, to live within their own enthralling horizons. So let me offer you a sobering, but I hope exhilarating thought: God never meant there to be a church in Islington; God meant there to be an Islington in the church.

In the eighth stanza of that curious and beautiful poem, Psalm 119, we read of the servant of the word, the poet, as one engaged in perpetual travel. Like the ancient Levites who had no landholdings, he declares, *My landholding is the Lord; for I have promised to keep your words.* Like the pilgrims who travelled every year to Jerusalem, he says: *I have sought thy face with all my heart; be gracious to me according to thy promise.* He has studied his route, planned his journey, wasted no time: *I have considered my way, and turn my feet to thy testimonies. I hasten and do not delay to keep thy commandments.* He has run into delays, but presses on: *The cords of the wicked ensnare me, but I do not forget thy law.* He has risen from his hotel bed in the small hours for an early start: *At midnight I rise to praise thee because of thy righteous ordinances.* He has found travelling companions of one mind with him: *A companion am I of all who fear thee, of those who keep thy precepts.* And then at the climax, where we expect him to reach the goal of his travels, Jerusalem, he discovers that his journeying is endless, for the whole world is where the Lord makes himself known: *Thy steadfast love fills the earth, O Lord; thy statutes do thou teach me.*

These are the terms in which I have spoken to you of the ministry in which I have engaged now for more than thirty years past, and your Vicar for a quarter-century. Forgive me for glorifying that ministry! It is certainly not to glorify either him or me. Indeed, I sometimes feel that only now, as in the course of nature my bodily energy grows weaker, do I begin to see the extraordinary scope and promise of it. Least of all is it to denigrate that other ministry, the ministry of settling the local church, of rooting, grounding, and establishing, the ministry of constant care and attention to neighbourly realities, purging tradition to fit it for mutual service, deepening familiarity into costly charity, strengthening bonds of affection that they may bear the communion of the Holy Spirit. The ministries God gives do not compete with one another, but strengthen one another and make one another more effective. The ministry of the word is to make the local ministry *rich with the treasures of the gospel.* The further that ministry reaches out, the more deeply the Islington that is within the church can put its roots down.

*   *   *

Eternal Word, issuing forth from the Most High in command and blessing, devise and direct among us speech which will answer God's speech, that binding ourselves in truthfulness and shared intelligence we may pour out for one another the gift you have hidden within us, and that we may be united with you in the highest word, which cries out, "Abba! Father!".

The Mission of God's Word

A New Message

Comfort ye, comfort ye my people!   ISAIAH 40:1

I quote from the Authorised Version, somewhat swallowing my pride. I am (I fear it is well known) unsound about the Authorised Version, thinking it not only primitive in scholarship but often unfelicitous in its command of the English language. Still, you won't do better for Isaiah 40:1.

> *Comfort ye, comfort ye my people! saith your God.*
> *Speak ye comfortably to Jerusalem, and cry unto her,*
>   *that her warfare is accomplished, that her iniquity is pardoned.*

Not only does it actually echo the commanding rhythm of the Hebrew original: *nah^amu nah^amu ammî.* It conveys what a modern translation is powerless to convey since modern English lacks a grammatical form for the plural imperative. And that happens to be the most important thing this prophet has to tell us about prophecy: that the echoing divine command, commissioning a message of reassurance and comfort to Jerusalem, is *in the plural,* addressed not to a single prophet but to an indeterminate number.

Prophecy has been the theme of Christian reflection on the Second Sunday in Advent ever since the formation of a common eucharistic

---

7th December 1997.

lectionary in the medieval Western church. *Whatever was written in former days was written for our instruction, that by steadfastness and by the encouragement of the Scriptures we might have hope.* So Saint Paul, in the passage read as the Epistle (Rom. 15:4), associated the *forward-looking* hope of Christian expectation with the *retrospective* reading of the Scriptures of the Jewish people. They had a meaning, too, for our times, upon whom the ends of the ages have come. In the new Church of England lectionary which came into effect last week we are invited to experience Advent at Matins in the company of Isaiah and that school of anonymous prophets whose work is bound up with his, the authors of most of the passages traditionally beloved at Carol Services. And today, when prophecy itself is our theme, our guide is the greatest of these anonymous successors, the figure christened by heavy-handed scholars "Deutero-Isaiah". We can't go on calling him that — it sounds so pompous and unfriendly! So let us take a leaf out of the book of another anonymous prophet, one known by the lead-word of his most famous prophecy, *Behold, I send my messenger* (Malachi) *before me.* We can call Deutero-Isaiah by the lead-word of his most famous prophecy, too. Let him be known as "Comfort-ye"! It has a pleasingly Puritan sound.

Comfort-ye, we must understand, lived in the mid-sixth century BC, after the cataclysm. When his parents were young and his grandparents at the height of their powers, the Babylonian armies burned Jerusalem to the ground and destroyed the kingdom of Judah as a political society, carrying away its ruling, priestly, and educated élites to the humiliation of exile by the Euphrates, hundreds of miles from their homes. As Comfort-ye grew up (no one is quite sure where, in Babylonia or among the ruins of Judaea) he was taught that this was no chance twist in the ever-unstable politics of the region, but the purpose of Israel's wrathful God, who had struggled for generations for the obedience of his people and had consistently given them detailed circumstantial warnings through his servants the prophets. And about the prophets he learned this, too: that at the last, when disaster fell about their heads and all their terrible predictions came to pass, they had had one final message: the calamity, though total, was not ultimate. After seventy years, said Jeremiah, God would visit his people. And now, for the first time since those traumatic happenings, geopolitical turmoil visited the Near East again. Babylon faced its last weeks of power before the assaults of its vassal,

Cyrus of Persia. To Comfort-ye it seemed that fulfilment was near. The message must go out: *Your God is coming.*

But could there still be a prophet now? The great prophets had been persons of public weight. They had stood confrontationally before kings as accredited interpreters of world-events; in the city-gate they challenged and aroused popular sentiment about laws and customs and politics. They performed their message with drama and with music, assisted by a troupe of followers and watched by crowds who flocked around them as crowds flock around entertainers. There were no kings now, no gate, no crowds. Where was the troupe of followers to be found? Where was the social support to provide a prophet and his followers a livelihood? To think of being a prophet in those days must have been like someone in our time thinking of being a powerful nobleman like the First Duke of Marlborough. The role does not exist. There is no social space for such a thing. The making of Judah's history by the spokesmen of the Most High was in the past. What remained now was only to record and reflect on the history that had been made. In Comfort-ye's day historical interpretation had passed, once and for all it seemed, out of the hands of actors into the hands of historians. His was an age of books. From it there comes the great narrative of Israel's past, the Books of the Kingdoms. But how could a people be aroused to the new moment simply by reading historians?

And then there was the question of the call. Each of the great prophets had pointed to a moment of vocation and authorisation, a vision in which God revealed the meaning of the times and sent him out upon his difficult way. Isaiah beheld the throne of God in the temple in the year that King Uzziah died. Jeremiah saw an almond tree two years before King Josiah launched his great reform. Ezekiel even laid claim to such a vision in Babylonia, though that was before Jerusalem fell. Those great vocational dramas brought the personality of the prophet before the public. They imprinted his identity upon their minds. But Comfort-ye comes before us anonymously. And that is not the result of some accident of transmission, tearing off a title, perhaps, from a scroll, so that the work got copied out incongruously at the back end of Isaiah. It is the prophet's self-conscious and deliberate mode of presenting himself. Prophecy in his time must be quite different, independent of personality and social role. Independent also, perhaps, though this is less clear, of dramatic presentation, more like pure poetry. Yet it must still declare the great event as it unfolds, and to prove itself it must show its continuity with the great prophetic legacy. One of Isaiah's most dramatic gestures was to seal up a scroll with a prophecy written on it and hand it to his disciples with the instruction to hide it away until the time was right. Comfort-ye's dramatic gesture is to open a scroll containing one of the newly compiled collections of Isaiah's words, and then solemnly to add his own compositions to it.

There is, then, no call-narrative. Generations of readers have felt the want of one, even back in pre-Christian times when the Old Testament was first translated into Greek. Comfort-ye wrote, apparently, *A voice says, 'Cry!' Another says, 'What shall I cry?'* And the translator, followed by most translators afterwards, wrote: "And *I* said, 'What shall I cry?'" Probably wrongly; but even if the translator was right, that is not much of a prophetic commission. This great overture with which the prophet begins his work is almost stubborn in its refusal to conform to what we expect of an opening gesture. In a Kierkegaardian mood we might call it "a non-visionary prologue in place of a call-narrative and without authority". Nothing is seen. Nothing is said to the prophet personally. There is just this sequence of voices, one after another, voices that he overhears, passing a message on like a chain of runners. *Comfort ye, comfort ye . . . !* says the first. And the next, *Prepare ye the way of the Lord in the desert! Cry!* says the third. *What shall I cry?* asks the fourth. *All flesh is as grass,* says the fifth. And then at the very end of the sequence a messenger is named. And here is a most puzzling moment, which actually contains the solution to the puzzle of the sequence of voices. "Zion", the city of Jerusalem, is to stand on her hilltop and proclaim, so that all her dependent towns and villages may hear. But didn't the first voice say, *Speak comfortably to Jerusalem?* The addressee must become the messenger! The comforted must become the comforter! And her message is, *Your God is coming!*

See, then, what has happened to prophecy. Now, the whole people has become a prophetic people. Jerusalem has become a prophetic city. But to whom, then, is the prophecy addressed? If all are prophets, who will be hearers? Comfort-ye never tires of telling us. The coastlands, the nations, the ends of the earth: they are to hear the message! God's great restorative act is not for this people only but through them touches the

The Mission of God's Word

world. And that is why the proclamations of Israel's prophets are proclamations to us, too. That is why we read them in Advent as our preparation for celebrating the Nativity. It is not that there lies encoded in Ancient Near-Eastern documents a secret message only to be understood six centuries later. It is that the nation whose experiences they interpret is *itself* God's prophetic message to us. Its role in history was to embody the message of the judging and restoring grace of God to all mankind, and so to prepare the way for the coming of God in judgment and grace. Jerusalem is comforted; Jerusalem comforts; therefore we, too, take comfort. Jerusalem is told to look for her God, and cries out that he is coming; therefore we, too, may look for her God coming to us.

Your God is coming! This message now takes precedence over all other possible prophetic messages. When Jeremiah was commissioned, he was *set over nations and over kingdoms, to pluck up and to break down, to destroy and to overthrow, to build and to plant.* He would hold the tumultuous rise and fall of nations in his hand. Not so Comfort-ye. His message is almost detached in its view of such things. *All flesh is as grass, and all its beauty is like the flower of the field. The grass withers, the flower fades, when the breath of the Lord blows upon it.* Their growth, their grandeur, their falling away is as predictable as grass in spring which scorches under the sirocco. Comfort-ye has a view of the cyclical, law-bound character of great events. He does not look to them to disclose anything new. All but for one thing: *the word of the Lord endures for ever.* That is the word of promise, the word of God's coming to his people. That is what now gives shape and meaning to the unfolding of history. Everything is focussed upon that. *Behold the Lord God comes with might, and his arm rules for him, and his recompense before him. He will feed his flock like a shepherd.* Here is the goal of all world history, the yearning of Israel and of the nations.

At one level Comfort-ye was a *true* prophet in the great tradition of Israel's true prophets. Like them he read the history of his times and got it right. For we should never forget that the high standing of prophecy in Israel grew from an almost astonishing record of getting things right. That is one of those stubborn facts about ancient Israel which our scepticism or belief has simply to take the measure of. They didn't *all* get it right, of course; the record does not conceal interpretative conflicts among prophets, between "false" and "true". And it didn't come out as they said all at once; Jeremiah lamented bitterly that he had been announcing the fall of Jerusalem for nearly forty years before it happened. But happen it did, and in the manner that he said it would. And what Comfort-ye said would happen, did happen. Cyrus the conqueror sent exiled peoples back to their homes, and Judah took up its national life again.

Looked at from another angle, though, Comfort-ye may seem the most doubtfully successful of all the prophets. Yes, there was the Decree of Cyrus and the community of returning exiles resettling in Jerusalem and Judah. Butt nothing could make it seem like the triumphant and world-renewing event that he described. The actual story of the returned community is something of an anti-climax after what he taught us to anticipate: an uphill struggle, often frustrated by hostile neighbours and by fruitless tensions between rigorists and compromisers in the community. In the next century Ezra still complains of political dependence upon Persia, *Behold we are slaves this day; in the land that thou gavest to our fathers. . . . behold we are slaves* (Neh. 10:36). And, of course, the restored community never held more than a proportion of the Jews in the Near East. There were those — and their voices are clearly heard within the Psalter — who never returned, never lived in the Holy Land thereafter.

Yet we would not have grasped the point if we thought that this ambiguous outcome seriously compromised Comfort-ye's announcement. He was looking for a *return,* but not for a *restoration.* His interest in this last step in Israel's sacred history was not that it should pave the way back to a glorious *status quo,* back to the days when David could boast that he ruled from the Mediterranean to the Upper Euphrates. It was simply that God's act of faithfulness to his people should be an ensign to the nations, a light to the Gentiles. Israel's history needed this last act as a *message,* a sign of the coming of God to the whole world. The great model-history itself, from Exodus to Second Exodus, was essentially completed at that point. The future lay with the sending of that message *out.* This was a prophetic history, and Israel's role was to proclaim it and make it comprehensible. No longer actors in events as they transpired, the prophets of the future would be poets and preachers, celebrating events already achieved. And that was why prophets of the future often imitated this prophet's self-imposed anonymity.

The Mission of God's Word

When as Christians, and probably as Gentile Christians, we read him as a prophet of the Incarnation, we prove the truth of his conviction that the coming of God to Israel was to be a light to the nations. Yet we must take our *own* responsibility for affirming that this coming touched Gentile history in the birth of a Jewish baby in Bethlehem. It was not his vocation to know of that or send us coded messages about it. We stand in no need of such messages. But we do stand in need of prophecy, of the account of God's working in history that tells how and where to look for its fulfilment. He tells us we shall find it by listening to the Jew, who speaks to us out of the deepest suffering yet triumphantly of the faithfulness of God, comforting his people, bringing their long struggle to an end, forgiving all their sin.

The Intruders

That the Gentiles should be fellow-heirs,
and of the same body.

EPHESIANS 3:6

The wise men seem so inevitable that we fail to see that they are really intruders. Imaginatively, we identify with them. "We three kings of Orient are", the Epiphany Collect, T. S. Eliot's *Journey of the Magi* all treat them as a symbol of our own spiritual pilgrimage to "the fruition of the godhead". But imagine yourself for a moment at the receiving end of their enquiries, as they barge into a Jewish pastoral idyll which is none of their business and which they do not understand. They put the wrong question at the wrong moment to the wrong person, hopelessly confused by Hellenistic political theology and astrology, and the result is tragedy. The story ought to be an object-lesson in the importance of not meddling.

We depend on people knowing what is and is not their business. Society grows for itself a kind of network of membranes which separate one set of concerns from another, create sheltered areas of shared responsibility, and facilitate diversity and complexity. These membranes are essential if anything valuable is to develop, like walls in a garden that protect and support the plants that could never grow on an open moor. They protect us from social exposure, which is to say, shame. A society that was entirely open — everything equally accessible to view from ev-

---

6th January 1991.

The Mission of God's Word

erywhere — would be bleak, barren, and intolerably aggressive. A subtle code of manners protects distinctions, not necessarily of value or worth, but simply of difference, marking off what can be said here, among friends, from what can be said there, among strangers. There is nothing prejudicial about that, though, of course, it can become degenerate and corrupt. Without a sense of "at home" and "abroad", we can never go anywhere. A refusal to acknowledge the difference between fellow-countrymen and foreigners would not mean better treatment for foreigners. Better see a foreigner as a foreigner! Better find him interesting and instructive! Otherwise you will see him as a failed specimen of the human race who has never learned how to behave!

Now, religion provides invaluable material for building these thin membrane-walls that separate one context of communication from another. Nothing so gently and unprejudicially stamps groups of people with their marks of belonging than the ritual, the liturgy, the style of service they feel at home in. Here is the best shelter for what is distinctive, tender, and noble in our aspirations, for what secures us at the centre of our beings. Under the shelter of religious particularity much that is great and wonderful can grow.

But what is that noise of bulldozers and dynamite? Who is breaking a gaping hole in the venerable old walls? Who has cut, obscenely straight, a motorway across the delicate tissue of hedgerows and fields? Alas, God has! It is Epiphany, the disclosure of the Jewish Christ to the Gentiles! The oh-so-sensitive, delicate, unprejudiced awareness of the appropriate communication is jarred, painfully, stridently, by this monstrous cosmic tactlessness, *that the Gentiles should be fellow-heirs, and of the same body.* This is mixing incompatibles with a vengeance!

On this day the worldwide Anglican Communion begins what it has dedicated as a Decade of Evangelism. Now, I assume that this word carries negative connotations with many of us, suggesting crass, heavy-handed attempts to herd people into religious faith and observance. And my first duty is to tell you that your worst fears are justified. Evangelism means sharing the good news of Christ, and that means breaking down the membrane walls that distinguish "us", for whom and among whom it is appropriate to discuss faith, from "them", with whom it is inappropriate for us to discuss faith. Yet, if we can brace ourselves for the shock of exposure, we can learn that evangelism is not as we feared it might be after all. It does not mean airlifting individuals out of the camp of the religiously untouched into the camp of the participants, though sometimes it may have that effect, which is not in itself a bad one. It means realising that the distinction between the two groups has *already* been breached, that the Spirit who attests Christ has pushed through this wall, has claimed the untouched as well as the participants, so that we have only to follow in our speech, to include all, since all have been addressed by God. No more discipline of the arcane! No more value-free, neutral ground!

I recall an occasion at the end of a rather winey dinner when a fellow-diner embarrassed me in front of the company by leaning across the table, reasonably drunk, and asking that I should explain to him how to find God. *How inappropriate!* I thought. Surely he cannot be a serious enquirer, raising the question at that moment and in those circumstances! On the contrary: it was the proof of his seriousness that he couldn't wait for the right moment and the right manner, and the question was simply whether I could match his, and God's, sense of urgency!

Pray, I beg you, for the Decade of Evangelism, and that we may all learn some of that mighty freedom which is God's own freedom; that we may recognise the opening of mankind to God wherever we may see it, may greet it joyfully in however unexpected a form, and speak to it of the young child of Bethlehem. Pray that a new generation of nosey wise-men and insensitive enquiring Gentiles may be rewarded, and that our walls may be rebuilt to accommodate them!

The Mission of God's Word

The Witness

Baptism of J—> we can look @ baptism as a divine action a human act, but in the baptism of J they are one single dimension. It is here the unity of his 2 natures come together. He is a human being who is finite & ∴ requires baptism, & he is G, & ∴ baptises with fire.

*I have seen, and have born witness that this
is the Son of God.*

JOHN 1:34

There are four Gospels, but only two tell of Jesus' birth at Bethlehem in the days of Herod the king, only one of the wise men led by a star to bring gifts to the manger. But all four tell of Jesus' coming to the bank of the Jordan, where John was baptizing; all tell of the Spirit like a dove descending, and of the heavenly voice in witness. Here we are at the very heart of Epiphany. For "Epiphany" is a disclosure, an appearance that breaks in upon our visual field, "dawns on us", as we say. All the evangelists tell of the epiphany by the Jordan; but Saint John tells of it in a different way.

What was disclosed on Jordan's bank? What did they go out into the wilderness to see? A prophet calling for repentance? A craftsman's son professing his allegiance to a movement of national and spiritual renewal? All this, but much more. For a moment the world's Creator drew the veil back from his face: the divine Spirit alighted on the Son, the Son was acknowledged by the Father. They saw one in whom the godhead declared himself, one in whom what may be known of God is known, one from whom nothing that may be known of God is missing. God acknowledging, God attesting, God self-acknowledged, self-attested. They saw the glory of God in tri-unity.

8th January 2006.

The Witness

is the baptism of J one of the key moments of the Gospel story, on a par w

19

And what else did they see? Here we must beware of rushing ahead too fast. We should like to say: they saw the glory of *man* disclosed, as the glory of God was disclosed; they saw the partner of the divine presence stepping out into the world with a new confidence and a new mission. And we may say that, for it is true. But we may not say it yet. Great heresy is great truth gulped down too quickly, ultimate things arranged in penultimate order, vision that cannot abide the disciplines of seeing. What they saw was the glory of God disclosed in a *definite man;* they saw Jesus of Nazareth, carpenter's son and Son of God. No divine presence, no perfect humanity, could be as disturbing as that. God known in the face of the anointed saviour of the race? Certainly. The pious had been looking for it. God known in the face of Jesus? We can hear the scornful response, *Can any good thing come out of Nazareth?* Here is the scandal over which faith chokes, the scandal of particularity. Someone who stood behind us in the queue, someone our second cousins played with as a boy, some ignorant chance-person. How can we see God's presence in the world, how can we see transformed humanity, man's holy partnership with God, in such a banality? And so they saw it, but did not see it.

One person, at least, saw it. His cousin, the Baptist, who declared, *I have seen, and have born witness that this is the Son of God.* And in St. John's Gospel the whole drama of Jesus' disclosure is shown us indirectly by way of what the Baptist saw and witnessed. It is as though John the Evangelist shrank from the suggestion that unseeing, uncomprehending eyes could simply look on the self-disclosure of God the Trinity and hear the attesting voice of God. What the synoptic evangelists tell is what was there to be seen and heard: the Father's voice from heaven, the descent of the Spirit like a dove, the anointed Christ rising from the water of baptism. But John focuses our attention upon how that seeing is effected. *No one has seen God at any time,* we can hear him saying, *the only Son, he who is in the bosom of the Father, has made him known.*

How it is seen, and by whom it is seen — for not every passing stranger on the banks of the Jordan sees and hears what takes place there, though there may be much to be seen and heard. *Some said it thundered,* as John comments on another voice from heaven. For the Son who is to be seen and will make the godhead known God has appointed one to see him, a witness. Jesus claims never to speak about himself

The Mission of God's Word

alone; there is always someone to bear witness alongside him. Sometimes it is Moses, sometimes the prophets; at the end of the Gospel it is the apostles. But at the beginning there is only one whom it can be, one appointed precisely for the task. *There was a man sent from God whose name was John.*

When Christians use the word "Epiphany" to describe the coming of Jesus, they are speaking not only about what dawned upon the world at that moment in history, but on how it dawned. In the New Testament the word is not often used, on four occasions, to be precise, of which three refer to Jesus' second coming to judge the earth, and only one to his first coming. But a word is no more than a word. The idea contained in it is constantly present in other words and groups of words. It is expressed by St. John in his Prologue: *we beheld his glory, glory as of the only Son of the Father.* And it is expressed in his account of the disclosure by the Jordan: *I saw the spirit descending as a dove from heaven and resting upon him.*

We can recognise and identify people and events in rather different ways. There are things we can identify because we have known them before. There are things we can identify because we can infer from other things we have known what they must be. And there are things that identify themselves to us, that open our eyes to see them. Epiphany speaks of a way of recognising of this third type, inseparable from *this* event, the disclosure of the Son of God.

We step off a train and walk from the platform into the ticket hall. Amid the crowd of people waiting there, one is familiar: we have seen that face and figure, and have heard that voice innumerable times. Identification is immediate. We don't ask for proofs, because the person waiting there is one we have known. And that is not how Jesus was identified as Son of God, not by us, not by John the Baptist, not by anybody.

On another occasion we walk into the ticket hall and see a face that is vaguely familiar; but when we hunt in our memory for previous meetings, we draw a blank. We recall that we once heard that the friend we have come to visit had an older sister living in the city. We heard that his family were powerful figures in city politics. Here is a woman with elegant streaks of grey in her hair, with a commanding bearing, eyeing us questioningly. We leap to a possible conclusion: has his sister come to meet us? Fragments of experience, none of which would support the conclusion on its own, come together; but there is only the measure of probability that the evidence allows, so we look for proof; we approach and ask, Are you by any chance Gregory's sister? And that is how Jesus may be identified as the Son of God, at first, by us. We have the witness of John the Baptist; we have the witness of the apostles; we have the witness of Moses and the prophets. All the elements of what we have known about him come together; they justify our making an approach in tentative faith. More immediate experience will follow; for the beginning, to lead us in, we depend on witnesses.

But what are the witnesses we depend on worth? If *we* are to make our hesitant way towards the Saviour on their testimony, must there not be a different and more direct way which they have taken? Otherwise it would be an infinite regress, everyone relying on somebody else's testimony. There must be a moment when recognition begins.

So imagine, finally, that we walk from the train into the ticket hall, and before we can recognise anybody, someone comes up to us. The Vice-Chancellor has sent him, he declares, as he promised in his letter that he would; his name is Jonas; he is in charge of the arrangements, and will chair the first meeting; he will now escort us to our hotel, and if we will allow him to take our bags and step this way, there is a car waiting outside. Of course, we yield. We have forgotten what the Vice-Chancellor said in his letter, and we didn't bring it with us to consult. We were not expecting to be met. Yet we are in no position to question whether the name of this tall, energetic man is what he says it is, nor whether he actually is the Vice-Chancellor's emissary. No knowledge of anybody's name or any features from our experience can be the slightest use in assessing the claim of this man to take us in charge and whisk us off to a place we do not know. All we can say is, it hangs together. We receive the impression that he makes on us, his claims for himself, his name, his features and appearance, his instructions and advice, his solicitude for our comfort, all as a whole. The identification takes place in one leap, not by inference or demonstration from things known to things unknown. Yet the whole content of what we identify is new and unprepared for. Its authority does not derive from any judgment we may make. It derives from its own self-attestation. It is a case, as one theologian has described it, of "seeing the form", receiving the whole picture, in which detail hangs together with detail.

The Mission of God's Word

I did not know him, John the Baptist declares — provoking the usual questions about how he could not know the man St. Luke says was his cousin. But it is not that he did not know his cousin, but that he did not know his cousin as the Son of God. And the man who did not know Jesus as the Son of God became the witness that he is the Son of God. How? There was more than one element in it. He heard the voice he knew as God's, the voice that had sent him off on his own ministry of baptism. He saw the Spirit descend on Jesus and rest on him. But he brought no prior knowledge of his own. And so he says, *I have seen.* "Seeing" is the word that brings the elements together. The very essence of "seeing" is taking things in as a whole. Nothing, in this world or out of it, has been really "seen" unless it has come together before someone's gaze in this way. To see only disjointed bits is simply not to see the thing at all. The moment cohered; it imposed itself upon John's mind, the whole form, appearance, meaning, and authentication all at once. And that is the only way, if you think about it, that anybody could possibly witness the disclosure of God. There is no starting point from which you could reach such a conclusion. It is genuinely new. It can be grasped only by letting it take hold and impose itself upon the categories of the understanding. Thought cannot *lead up to* that moment; it can, and must, *run out* from it.

No wonder the Evangelist says of his namesake the Baptist, *There was a man sent from God!* For his task of witness, of seeing what there was to be seen, was not a task that someone could simply undertake for himself. It was given to whom it was given. But can this way of seeing be given to anyone *after* John? Is he a witness of such a kind that no one else can be? Are the rest of us driven back on simple faith without sight? Or may we, in some sense, come to see what there is to be seen?

The Baptist says, in a rather witty play of words, that the one who comes after him went before him, because he was — shall we dare to try to capture the joke in English? — his *foreman.* The "before" and the "after" of sacred time are gathered up in an overarching relation of sovereignty in which the Word of God is "first". John's witness is in time. That is why it is irreplaceable. He stood there watching when the one who came after him was revealed. So we cannot set ourselves free of what John, and only John, can tell us. And that is the meaning of the slightly daunting phrase, "the authority of Scripture". Simply, there is no possible way for us to grasp the self-giving of God in history unless we rely on the historical witnesses God sent. There is no bypassing faith, no claiming a sight of Christ that enjoys its own point of critical perspective on what they have told us. We cannot and must not listen to those who claim to pit Christ against the testimony borne to him by his apostles — for there is no other Christ than the apostles' Christ, except that will o' the wisp of our own sentimental religious imaginations to which each generation is always more ready to lend credit than it deserves. Downstream from the apostles' view of Christ we are, downstream we remain. Yet that relationship, inescapable and irreversible as all historical relationships are, is not the last word. When all that must be said has been said, there is an inner kinship between faith and sight, a latent equality between the Baptist and ourselves. Christ is our common foreman. Faith grows into sight, and as it takes root in us, so it outgrows its beginnings as a mere conclusion from premises, the result of a train of thought. It becomes the basis on which we live, the shape that our mind gives to new experience. The form comes together in new ways, because Christ is present even though the Baptist is past. We shall never stand in his shoes on the banks of the Jordan, but we can, here on the ever-clammy banks of the Thames, see what is there to be seen: the reality and power of Christ unfolding in a demonstration of his presence and his lordship. Sight must be given us, as all the great founding phenomena of experience are given us, and to prepare for it what we must do is to attend to the testimony, to think outwards from it. Yet sight *is* given to us; and it is given to us to witness. For this is the one who comes after as well as before us, the one who baptizes in the Holy Spirit.

Travelling to Jerusalem

Lo, your king comes to you; triumphant and
victorious is he, humble and riding on an ass,
on a colt the foal of an ass.   ZECHARIAH 9:9

The event recalled for us every Palm Sunday, the triumphal entry of Jesus into Jerusalem, comes at the climax of a *journey*. Of the four evangelists it is St. Luke who makes the most of that fact. He divides his
Gospel into two unequal parts: in the first he collects all the material
he has taken from Saint Mark; in the second and larger part he distrib-
utes all the other accounts he knows of Jesus' ministry around Jesus' final journey from Galilee to Jerusalem. It begins as early as chapter 9
with the words, *When the days drew near for him to be received up, he set
his face to go to Jerusalem* (9:51), and subsequently no fewer than ten
times the evangelist reminds us of this context. Jesus refuses to be dis-
tracted by Samaritan inhospitality; he declines to be frightened into
haste or hiding by news that King Herod has ordered his arrest, for *it
cannot be that a prophet should perish other than in Jerusalem!* The
drama heightens as he passes through Jericho, approaching the long
final climb, and then comes the most powerful stroke: as the city itself
comes into view, the triumphal progress is interrupted and Jesus stops
to weep at the sight of it. For Saint Luke everything has hung upon
that journey. Jesus is like an Atlantic wave that travels a thousand

9th April 2006, Palm Sunday.

miles across the surface of the ocean to hurl itself upon the indifferent cliffs of Kerry.

What is this journey for? To liberate and to deliver; to bring good news to a beleaguered city. From a hilltop city you can see people coming, and the imaginations of Judah's prophets were captured by the thought of an approach that would herald God's settlement of the unending crisis in Jerusalem's affairs. *How beautiful upon the mountains are the feet of him who brings good tidings!* (Isa. 52:7). *Upon your walls, o Jerusalem, I have set watchmen . . . Say to the daughter of Zion, "Behold your salvation comes!"* (Isa. 62:6, 11). *Blessed is he who comes in the name of the Lord*, ran the Hillel Psalm (Ps. 118:26), which the crowds sang as they accompanied Jesus along that road by which millions of pilgrims over the centuries had approached the city. But the evangelists, recalling this, heard the echo of another text, read to us this morning: *Lo, your king comes!*

But it is also a journey to trial and to judgment. As the journey has gone forward, the tension has built up. A challenge is to be issued to Jerusalem, and a response, perhaps a violent one, to be expected. How will the hilltop city receive the one sent with good news of her redemption? Will she arise and shine? Will she climb to the top of the heights among which she is sited, and cry to the cities of Judah, *Behold your God!?* Or will she, as she has so often before, refuse the word, turn against the messenger, and so encompass her own doom? Two judgments are to be given in Jerusalem: a judgment by the city on the one who comes, and a judgment given by God upon the city.

As often in prophetic expectation, this approach is marked by large accompanying crowds, celebrating the pilgrim feast and their liberation: *"Lift up your eyes round about and see; they all gather together, they come to you; your sons shall come from far, and your daughters shall be carried in the arms"* (Isa. 60:4). Jesus seems often to have moved around the countryside with such a train, cumbrously but in a mood of high popular excitement, and especially on this last journey, where his passage through the towns on his route became an occasion of excited spectacle. Disciples go ahead to make arrangements and report on the reception to be expected. *Jesus of Nazareth is passing through!* they tell blind Bartimaeus as he sits by the roadside in Jericho, while Zacchaeus has sufficient warning to find himself a perch where he can view the great event in comfort.

The Mission of God's Word

It is what happens to those crowds that tends to occupy our minds on Palm Sunday. Fickle crowds! we say. Melting away before the confrontation, leaving their celebrated master to his solitary witness! "Sometime they strew his way and his sweet praises sing . . . then Crucify! is all their breath . . ." I think that is a little severe. The crowds that escorted Jesus, as St John is careful to explain, were a mixture of two kinds of people: there were those already in the city as Passover pilgrims, who came out to meet him, and there were those that came with him, at least from as far as Bethany. These pilgrim crowds were not the regular city crowds which the authorities were to rouse against Jesus. One way or another they were from out of town, like a farmers' demonstration in a French city.

However that may be, at the journey's climax Jesus' challenge had to enter a phase of solitary combat. This, too, was of the essence of prophetic expectation. *Who is this that comes from Edom, in crimsoned garments from Bozrah? I have trodden the wine press alone, and from the peoples no one was with me* (Isa. 63:1-4). Why is this? What is the isolation demanded of the messenger as he reaches his goal? Just look at what that goal is! The city? Yes, but within the city one building in particular: the temple! All our witnesses tell us that on the day of his entry Jesus headed straight there. This was, or should have been, the heart of the people's life, the place where it offered worship, the source of God's word of guidance issuing forth from Jerusalem to the farthest corners of the land. But it was the house of God that had become a den of thieves! As he enters the temple, the relation between Jesus and the crowds changes. There he assumes authority. He takes his seat in the temple precinct, in despite of the authorities, to teach. Teach as he has always done, but from a new position, and no longer to a self-selected crowd of ready hearers, a gathering of the spiritually hungry, the physically afflicted, the economically impoverished, the rural radicals, but to a mixed urban crowd, led by the contenders for authority. Here it is not enough to be party leader. Here in the temple he embarks upon his hardest task: to bring the people to confront itself and its identity. And here, consequently, he must stand alone, for he must reconcile his rural enthusiasts and his urban despisers, those two very different perspectives on life and nationhood, into one people serving one God in one house of prayer.

For the task of delivering Israel was not an *external* but an *internal* task. For Jesus it was not — and never had been, so far as we can judge — a question of marshalling forces to throw the Roman occupation out. To empower Israel meant mending its internal relations, and supremely mending its relations to God. Israel's self-identity was not an enclosed identity, but an identity with God's purposes for the whole world. And for that to be realised the great work of representation had to be accomplished. The one who lived and taught *for many* must be together with them and at the same time apart from them. He must step forward. His own singular identity must mediate between their numerousness and the unity God calls them to. And that is why the multitude seems to fall away, so that Jesus may take up his exposed role of representing and reconciling all. That is why the struggle of the next days is undertaken in painful solitude. *Strike the shepherd, scatter the sheep,* he quoted to his disciples in Gethsemane.

The words that immediately follow that fragment of quotation are these: *But after I am raised up, I will go before you to Galilee.* Standing apart is not the end of the matter. Once again there must be going-before. The journey that came in liberation to Jerusalem must be concluded, the work of reconciliation done, in a triumphant journey outwards with Jesus at the head. Not only does the deliverer come to Jerusalem to tell her of God's victory; Jerusalem herself must get up into a high mountain, send the news out to the cities of Judah, lead the triumph into the countryside. And that is why we must never succumb to the temptation to be pathetic or tearful on Palm Sunday. The tone of pathos, the accent of resignation, the sense of bitter irony at the overshadowing of joy by suffering, has to be restrained, kept within the framework of God's final plan: *Out of Jerusalem shall come deliverance.* Our palm crosses are given to us as a sign of victory. And after the resurrection the crowds did go up to Galilee and meet the risen Lord — more than five thousand, Paul informs us, who saw him there at one time.

Jesus' journey, his solitary confrontation with the forces of disobedience and his triumphant return, corresponds to an ancient paradigm, a long-known, long-expected pattern of divine redemption. It corresponds to it, but also, in the view of the first believers, fulfils it; it gives the decisive turn to it that means that it can no longer be repeated. The apologetic motif of fulfilled prophecy makes sense because repeated patterns need a single event to fulfil them. Believing in one God, active and caring for his world, we believe that God's actions serve a goal; they are not endlessly repetitive like the regularities of nature. His ways of acting are a way which leads to an end. History will reveal that way and lead to that end. Time is not a dimension in which we move forward and back, as we move forward and back in space. Time is history, shaped by the good will of a creator.

And precisely for this reason all earlier history takes on a new appearance for those who accompanied Jesus. Stories time-honoured and familiar from long repetition now gain a new and strange suggestiveness as seen from the climax to which they have led. In the course of this coming week at Evensong I shall be reading with you one of those ancient stories in just this way, alongside the story of the Passion, to see what light they shed on each other. It is the story of a journey undertaken by one whom God appointed to redeem the people, one who went ahead of them to prepare a place of safety, but whose deeper task was to effect a reconciliation — the story of Joseph.

But there is another set of analogies to consider. If all *previous* journeys of deliverance end in *this* journey, all *earlier* acts of reconciliation climax in *this* act, it is also true that this journey and this reconciliation changed the whole world into its own shape. In its wake there came a people that had journeyed with the Redeemer, had participated in the reconciliation. A journeying, reconciling people lives out the climactic journey, the decisive reconciliation, in a hundred thousand lesser journeys of reconciliation. Whenever we think of our lives as a journey — it is a common enough cliché — we attach ourselves, knowingly or unknowingly, to the pattern Jesus has given us, the form of living he has opened to us. And so there is something repeated, as Holy Week itself is repeated year by year, a pattern of obedience and conformity to the unrepeatable. In our repetition of the story over the next few days we shall find ourselves continually faced with the question of the shape of our own existence: whether we are, and how we may be, conformed to his sufferings and his accomplishment.

With the passion story, as with every aspect of Jesus' life, one can look at it from either of two angles: there is the divine character of the event, and there is the human character; it is a unique moment in God's action for the world's redemption, and it is a pattern for a fully human existence. No sufferings could be like those sufferings; yet all sufferings may be conformed to those sufferings. No love can ever redeem as that love redeemed; yet all love is called to reflect the redemptive power of that love. No one ever journeyed as Jesus journeyed, to carry the judgment of God into the holy city and to reconcile God's people; yet all our human journeying may and can be a reliving of that journey. *Lo, your king comes to you.* Come with him!

The Servant

Who could have believed what we have heard,
and to whom has the power of the Lord been revealed? ISAIAH 53:1

The Servant of the Lord appeared first at a distance, an observer's distance, in the third person: *Behold my servant. . . . He will make justice shine on the nations.* Then, as the prophet looked more closely, he became drawn into the Servant's role and identified with it, so that he spoke in the first person, *I gave my back to the smiters.* But now the possibilities for empathy fall away. The prophet stops short in appalled surprise, and resumes his third-person description: *Who could have believed what we have heard? His form, disfigured, lost the likeness of a man . . .*

Here is the point of what Jesus said to his disciples at the last supper, *Where I am going you cannot come!* We have spoken this week of following, of participating in the authority of the Servant. But there is a limit to that following, that participation. Authority is authorship; and authorship means coming first, which is always a task of solitude. He is, as the Epistle to the Hebrews likes to say, the "pioneer". As the Servant speaks to us with God's word, his word becomes our word; he draws us into it beside himself; he makes us a community of the word. Yet it is always *his* word first, *our* word second. He speaks what we may speak after and with him; we speak what he has already spoken for us.

But if there is solitude in coming first, there is solitude, too, in com-

---

2nd April 1999, Good Friday.

ing last. And that is the place of authority as well. The one who leads also rounds up. The one who speaks for a community must answer for it. Every challenge, every question that we face, comes back in the end to him. The Servant's speech takes responsibility. By telling the truth about good and evil it takes responsibility for the evil as well as the good. It will not brush it aside. We may shrug our shoulders, turn our backs and stride off in irritation; but if we do, we give up the attempt to tell the truth. No angry put-down ever told the truth about evil; for it refuses to stand in the place of responsibility. How can the Servant lead us into pure speech, except by speaking responsibly for our attitudes of arbitrary *un*-speech? How can we take his speech about God's peace and justice on our lips, unless he can give us speech about that *un*-peace and *in*-justice in which we stand? What are ideals, without self-criticism? By speech he has bound us to himself in the way of speech; by speech he has bound himself to us in our turning back from speech.

In P. T. Forsyth's wonderful phrase, the crucifixion is "the Great Confession", an articulate acknowledgment of all that unspeakable refusal of speech which has soured and stupefied the human race in every age. To call the cross "speech" is another paradox, of course. The Servant is silent. He did not open his mouth. Yet just as we may mask our violence by the pseudo-speech of demagoguery and lies, so he masks his speech in silence. For speech forms itself in the medium of silence, the true word becomes articulate in the withholding of a false one. Because he could have spoken for himself, by not speaking he spoke for others, binding himself to those who have nothing to say for themselves, taking responsibility for them, putting a word of confession in their mouths. "Du sprichts stillschweigend, Ja!", as we heard at the climax of Bach's wonderful Passion on Wednesday evening. "In silence saying, Yes!".

The chastisement of our peace is upon him. In that lapidary phrase the prophet sees why the Servant must be alone. He is to represent the hope of the new Israel; but he must represent the failure of the old Israel first. A new Israel is God's redemptive purpose; but a new Israel can only be a renewed Israel if it takes responsibility for the old. Otherwise it is merely a replacement. Gentile Christians early in the church's history failed to understand this. They thought that because the church was the new Israel, the old must be obsolete, discontinued. They saw the old Israel in Caiaphas, and never grasped that it was not Caiaphas who spoke

The Mission of God's Word

for the old Israel that day, but Jesus. The chastisement of Israel's peace was upon him. The old Israel could never be discarded by the new, but only renewed in it.

Behold, my servant shall prosper. As we come to the end of this week's meditations on the Servant, the prophet leads us back to where we began. The meaning of the Servant is nothing if not the triumph of authority. It was a *political* experience that prompted the prophet's searchings, the experience of many a displaced, disempowered people, that asked what could lie beyond the wall of force. It was a *political* answer that he gave, when he spoke of the triumph of the word spoken from God, in liberating and directing the nations. That triumph was won in the very citadel of arbitrary oppression, as speech took responsibility through prophecy. *The Lord took thought for his tortured Servant.* In that sentence suffering and triumph, passion and resurrection are bound together. Of course, there is still an opposition between them. It is not that torture *is* the Lord's thought for his Servant , or that death can be represented by some metaphysical sleight of hand as life. The Lord's thought reverses the torture, it overcomes death with life. Yet beneath the opposition there is a deeper unity. Things were as they seemed as Jesus hung upon the cross; but not only as they seemed. The cunning of mercy was at work there, so that things could not remain as they seemed. Deep in the rock of the tomb, you could find the roots of the tree of life. *To whom has the power of the Lord been revealed?* To those who have looked to see it at work in the desolation and death of his Servant.

Seeing the Risen One

You have not seen him, yet you love him. I PETER 1:8

Why was the resurrection of Jesus so difficult to see? Even the apostles saw him, as it were, on an occasional basis only, and found it hard to recognise him. And after the forty days — so short a time! — even they had to trust him without seeing him, just like the rest of us. Why should the resurrection have been so elusive?

It is difficult to see, because we are at the receiving end of what God has done. If a whirlwind sweeps across the valley, picks us up high in the air, carries us across the roofs of the city, and throws us down on the hill the other side, we shall not see very much of what is happening. If a car knocks us down in the road, we are unlikely to get a clear view of the model and the number plate. Now God has picked us up, God has knocked us over. When Jesus stood in the High Priest's judgment-hall, he was at our mercy. We blindfolded him, struck him on the cheek, and asked, "Who struck you?" But come Easter Day, he asks us, "Who struck you?" We once knew Christ "according to the flesh", as Saint Paul put it. We had him comfortably within our field of vision, and we looked him up and down. But it is not like that any longer, since the old has passed away and the new has come. Our relation to him has changed: we are the passive ones, we are held within his field of vision.

Praise to the God and Father of our Lord Jesus Christ, who gave us new

---

23rd April 1995.

birth! St. Peter cries. Perhaps, like me, you were brought up on the antique Authorised Version, hallowed in all places where they sing Samuel Sebastian Wesley: *who according to his abundant mercy hath begotten us again unto a lively hope....* Then came the Revised Standard Version, and turned it round: *we have been born anew to a living hope....* Our birth, our conversion, our baptism is the cause of our satisfaction. But the apostle never spoke or thought like that. Now the New English Bible has turned it back again, more literally and more faithfully: *he gave us new birth.* There we have it right: it is God's act, God's gift in the resurrection of his Son. The Father of Jesus, on whom he called in the Garden of Gethsemane, has been merciful. He has raised his Son from the grave. He has given us all new life.

The most difficult thing about Easter is learning to be at the receiving end, to be the object, not the subject, of what is going on. At Christmas we hasten to welcome the newborn King. In Lent we repent and impose a discipline upon ourselves. In Holy Week we reproach ourselves for our rejection of him. And at Easter it is all taken out of our hands. There is no initiative left to us — not even believing! Poor Thomas would have liked not to believe, but he had no say in the matter. There was Jesus, commanding him to believe. There was Thomas, believing despite himself. But perhaps, you say, there is a tiny corner left to us for our initiative; perhaps we can go one better than Thomas. *Blessed are those who have not seen, and yet believe,* said Jesus. Can we not, as it were, get in first and do our believing quickly, before faith is summoned from us by the objectivity of the resurrection reality? Theologians have come up with something they have been pleased to call "Easter faith". It is the new life of joy and belief within the Christian community that is so strong that it can do without the objective evidence of the resurrection and can just feed on its own internal reserves! But like so much that is pious and edifying, this Easter faith is not faith at all. Seeing or unseeing, faith happens when reality catches up with us from behind, overtakes us before we can execute our well-planned disposal of ourselves. The presence of the risen Lord and the new world of his resurrection catch us out, surprise us, find us unready, looking the other way.

Why is the resurrection difficult to see? Because it is more real than the world to which our perceptions are fashioned, within which we have learned to live and to observe. Imagine yourself lying paralysed on a bed in a small, dark sickroom. One day your nurse pulls back a blind that has covered a skylight in the ceiling, through which light rushes in. It tells you that there is a world out there, a world of sun, of fresh air, movement, growing plants. You can see none of them; but the light streaming into the room brings that whole world vividly to your awareness, a world you cannot get up and share in, but which is joyfully, painfully objective. *You are transported with a joy too great for words,* as Peter says. But the joy itself is not important; it is merely the subjective response. It is the world out there, forcing itself in on you though you cannot see it, which renews you and makes you part of its life. And with that life, hope; for you cannot be grasped by that world without its promising you, by anticipation, to become a part of itself.

There is one more resurrection appearance to come, and that will be the first complete resurrection appearance, when the risen Lord will be seen together with his risen world. Sense will follow sympathy. *He has given us new birth to a living hope.*

The Mission of God's Word

The Opening of the Kingdom

When thou hadst overcome the sharpness of death,
thou didst open the Kingdom of Heaven to all believers. TE DEUM

The secrets of God were laid bare to the universe as the risen Christ ascended to his Father's right hand. What God had whispered in the darkness was now shouted from the rooftops. The greatness of his mercy reached to the heavens and his faithfulness to the clouds, his glory was over all the earth. The divine triumph was now no distant dawn on the horizon, but filled the four quarters of the sky; it was no chrysalis of potentiality, but a flash of present splendour. There remained no further depths to the Father's good pleasure, nothing that he was hugging to himself. All was made explicit, all laid open for angels and men to adore. Jesus the captain of renewed humanity sat at the right hand of the glory of God the Father.

And yet precisely at the point where there is nothing further to be revealed, everything is hidden. The cloud hides Jesus from the disciples' sight. "'Tis only the splendour of light", we may sing, "hideth thee", but it hid him nonetheless, and we cannot penetrate it with mind or eye. All that manifest appearance of glory is paradoxically a disappearance. Indeed, the disappearance is the sign of the appearance. It is because Jesus is not here, not open to our view, that we know he is there, where all is open to view. It is because he has gone away that we know that the door

11th May 1986.

of our prison-house stands open, and we may go with him. About the Ascension everything is mysterious to us. The opening of God's secret is not, after all, an evacuation of the mystery. The sea is not drained out, so that the stones and sand and seaweed appear naked to the light of day; rather, we are led down into the depths like divers, so that the deep is shown to us as we are swallowed up in it. The mystery is all around us, impenetrable, even as we are permitted to penetrate it.

The Ascension brings us up against the boundaries of our spatial imagination. To what "above" did he ascend? By what "outside" is our time and space bounded? In what relation can we place Jesus at the right hand of the Father without (as Athanasius so wittily put it) setting the Father on his left? But such teasers for the imagination are only the opening feints in the arduous wrestling match to which our intelligences are summoned. What is the meaning of Christ's Ascension for our time, past and future? When the early church read in the Book of Daniel about the Son of Man coming in the clouds, they were prompted to look both backwards and forwards. Here, they said, is the key to that disappearing which marked the end of the forty days of Easter. But here, too, is that final appearing which is the other side of the disappearing, the universal appearing in which the whole world shall lie open before the glory of God. Yet there are not two comings of the Son of Man, but one. How can we grasp that this appearing is accomplished and still to be accomplished? And how can we understand our own times as poised between two moments in one climactic event which fulfils all God's promises?

More demanding still, how can we understand the relation of Christ's Ascension to what went before it? How can we who have rejoiced together at Easter, who have told each other of the triumph over death and of redemption completed, now celebrate this further moment of triumph? What can the mystery of the Mount of Olives add to the mystery of the empty tomb? Has the Easter gospel not said all that needs to be said? Or was that great appearing, after all, simply to end in disappearing, so that our joy in the returning Lord was merely a cunning way of coming to terms with his final absence? In seeking an answer to these questions I turn back today to the ancient, fifth-century hymn, the *Te Deum,* which we hear sung Sunday by Sunday. There is, in truth, more than one way in which the logic of the sequence of Easter and Ascension

The Mission of God's Word

can be explored, and this hymn does not offer us the only approach. But it offers us *an* approach, which will suffice for this morning: "When thou hadst overcome the sharpness of death, thou didst open the Kingdom of Heaven to all believers".

In the first place it interprets the Ascension as the *opening* of the Kingdom.

When we recite the great creeds, the deeds and sufferings of the Son of God are laid out for us in a series of main verbs, impressive in their cumulative narrative power: "He was conceived . . . and born. . . . He suffered . . . was crucified, died and was buried. He descended to the dead. On the third day he rose again. He ascended into heaven." In the *Te Deum* no such thing happens. The key moments of divine self-emptying and Paschal victory are packed away into subordinate clauses: "*when* thou hadst overcome the sharpness of death . . ." (or so runs the English translation; in the Latin the same effect is achieved with participial phrases). The main verbs do not offer a narrative, but an interpretation of the events: "thou didst not abhor . . . thou didst open the Kingdom of Heaven . . ." The Incarnation and Ascension assume especial importance for this author, since they illustrate the same thing. The eternal Son of the Father, to whom authority belongs, exercises his kingly right inclusively, to draw humanity within its sphere. He reaches out to take hold of the humblest moment of human existence, a moment so humble that some philosophers assure us airily that it cannot be thought of as human at all. And he leads humanity out of the bondage of death into the glory of God's kingly rule. His authority counts us in. And in the Ascension we see this as he *opens* the Kingdom of Heaven to us. *Lift up your heads, o ye gates, and be ye lift up, ye everlasting doors, that the king of glory may come in!* Yes, and bring with him in his triumphal train the whole race of humankind, the race which he has purposed to have within, not to leave outside, the Kingdom of his Father!

This moment is a universal moment, a moment for all. (The English translators added the word "all", but they were true to the spirit.) Christ opens the Kingdom of Heaven *to believers* — which is not a closed category (as when we advertise a scholarship which is open to sons of the clergy born in Herefordshire) but an open one (as with a scholarship for which all may apply). Each step along the way, of course, was universal in its implications. The flesh he bore was not only Mary's flesh, but our flesh. The temptations he fought were not merely those of the Judaean desert, but the temptations of everywhere. The death he died was not under Pontius Pilate alone, but under every blow of mortality. The body that rose from the tomb was not merely the crucified body, but all our bodies. Yet how are we so certain of this confident claim that it was "for all"? By what right do we claim a part in his steadfastness, his faithfulness, his mighty vindication? By right of the fact that God has exalted him to his right hand on high, has made him universal lord, lord of our temptations, our deaths and of our resurrections, too. *In putting everything in subjection under his feet, he left nothing outside his control* (Heb. 2:8). Nothing unsubdued, nothing rebellious, nothing dissonant, nothing merely apart. From this final moment the meaning of all that went before takes shape. His birth, ministry, death, and resurrection, all lead to this universal rule which willy-nilly, one way or the other, counts us into it.

Iudex crederis esse venturus. "We believe that thou shalt come. . . ." Of course he shall come! For the Ascension was never a mere going, which did not have the promise of a coming at its heart. The one who sits at the right hand of the Father is the one who *came,* to reach out and to take hold. His sitting is not a gesture of repose, not of aloof transcendence, but a constant authoritative presence to his redeemed creation. His coming is the law of the universe and of our human race. And that means that the form history takes, too, must acknowledge the authority that is his. Its empty randomness and wastefulness — worse, its pretensions to purpose and direction which turn out to be no more than projections of our lust for tyranny — these must yield to the destiny which God has in store for human history, to make the rule of Christ conspicuous. "Thou didst open the Kingdom of Heaven to all believers".

We observe, in the second place, that this opening, this universalising of Christ's reign is an opening of the Kingdom *of Heaven,* which is to say, of God. When we look, as we have looked all too wistfully and hopelessly in England these past eighteen months, for a break in the clouds and a sight of the sun, the sun we hope to see is the same sun we remember and have known from of old. That sun, we believe, is there behind the clouds, and its appearing — though something of a rarity for us — is a reaffirmation of what never ceased to be there. And so it is with the Kingdom of Heaven. The rule of God has always been there; it has always lightened the world; it has always presided over the direction

The Mission of God's Word

of history. Christ is the eternal Son of the Father, who did not begin to exercise authority for the first time on the day he was taken up from the Mount of Olives. The story of his coming to earth, his ministry, his passion and vindication, is not the story of how he *won* authority to rule, but of how he *exercised* the authority to rule that was his already. In this respect the *Te Deum* is a corrective to all the prejudices with which we naturally approach the Christian faith. Compressing the whole drama of Christ's earthly life into two short verses, it is content to celebrate the authority of the Son of God from everlasting to everlasting.

The second half of the hymn ("Thou art the king of glory, O Christ . . .") flows quite naturally, therefore, from the first. The Son, worshipped with the Father and the Holy Spirit by choirs of apostles, prophets, martyrs, and the holy church throughout all the world, exercises divine rule by drawing us human beings under its sway. The real significance of the story that the Gospels tell is not merely that it happened, but that its happening disclosed the changeless glory of what was always and irrevocably the case: God rules and extends his rule to quicken us in our begetting and resurrect us in our dying. Never was there another lord than the lord shown to us in the man from Nazareth. Other lords in plenty we have constructed in our fantasies, the cocoons of unreality which we have thrown round ourselves for protection from the real, only to discover that they have become our prisons. But as the Kingdom of Heaven is opened, they are shown up for what they were, shadows and imaginations, vanishing into empty air before the always-real. What is really new, as Milton tells us, is not the sun, but the dawn:

> So when the sun in bed,
> Curtained with cloudy red,
>   Pillows his chin upon an orient wave,
> The flocking shadows pale
> Troop to th' infernal jail,
>   Each fettered ghost slips to his several grave,
> And the yellow-skirted fays
> Fly after the night-steeds, leaving their moon-loved maze.

"We *believe* that thou shalt come . . ." Of course we "believe"! For what is it that will come, other than what is real? The one who, seated at the Father's right hand, is the Word through whom all things came to be? Therefore, again, his presence is the law of this universe and of our human race, a presence that has never been withdrawn but waits to be made explicit. In that profoundest order of things we have believed, for that alone has the reality to evoke our true belief. And in its future confirmation we continue to believe, because a history that defied reality would be simply unbelievable. In basing ourselves on this eternal solidity, which banishes our phantom fears for the future, we know the law of life. We set the trivial, the *Ersatz,* the anxious, away from us with just such confidence and satisfaction as one who discovers health food and gives up eating junk. In believing we allow the fullness of reality to grasp us as never before, though it is always the same reality that has grasped us before. "Thou didst open the Kingdom of Heaven to believers".

In the third place, we notice that the opening of Heaven discloses a *Kingdom,* a *rule* of reality, that is, an active sphere of authority, not some inert object which we can have at our disposal and deal with as we choose. This is, perhaps, the most difficult aspect of the Ascension to grasp, since we moderns lack the conception of what true authority is. We are all, it seems, frustrated anarchists, thinking the sole function of authority is to restrain us — necessarily, no doubt, but still distastefully. We have forgotten that authority liberates because it authorises. *I am a man under authority,* said the centurion to Jesus; and we expect him to go on, "My boss says to me, Go, and I go." But he says, *I say to this man, Go, and he goes.* For to be under authority is to be in authority. To be subject to its order is to be empowered to evoke order in the things around us. To be commanded is to be free to command. Authority spills over like one of those fountains with which Bernini and his contemporaries decorated the city of Rome. The more layers there are to catch the falling water, the more jets there are to pour it out again. The rule of God is that which at once commands and authorises us, which lays claim upon us and makes us free. The opening of the Kingdom of Heaven is the signal for mankind's empowerment, to act co-operatively in community, to act individually in fulfilment of personal vocation, to act commandingly over the wealth of natural goods, to act courageously in the face of natural perils, to act constructively in the presence of opportunity, to act believingly in the face of opposition, to act truthfully in the face of lies. From this moment all authority springs, and you and I will share that authority to the extent that we are subject to the one to whom *all authority is given in Heaven and upon earth.*

"We believe that thou shalt come *to be our judge*". Of course the ascended Lord must judge! For the reality he discloses is authoritative. It distinguishes substantial from insubstantial. It drives the sharpest possible division between what is true and what is untrue. It pronounces an authoritative No at the same time as it pronounces a decisive Yes: a No to all that is ungrounded, deceptive, and destructive of creation. The opening of the Kingdom means the judgment of the shadows and their servants — be they in ourselves or in the world about us. If it were not so, there could be no illumination, no resolution of ambiguity, misunderstanding, and deception. We would be forever what we are now, half closed to one another, a prey to doubts and suspicions of one another. And of ourselves, too! For did I ever fear another person's weakness or doubt another person's good will with the brooding anxiety with which I fear and doubt my own? For this reason we can cry with gratitude, following the English translation, "We believe that thou shalt come to be *our* judge"! Nothing less can liberate us from the oppression of the judgment we pass on ourselves and on each other. *Search me, o Lord, and know my heart! Try me and know my thoughts! And see if there be any wicked way in me, and lead me in the way everlasting!* (Ps. 139:23f.).

Yet the Latin says less than that, and more than that. "We believe that thou shalt come *as judge*". It suggests more, if it reminds us that the throne on which the Son of Man sits is not to be a solitary throne, but surrounded by the thrones of his saints who will judge the world. For this judgment is something he wills to share with mankind. It searches us out, not that we may be merely speechless under its scrutiny, but that we in turn may be enabled to search out all things. *Then shall I know as I am known,* said Saint Paul (1 Cor. 13:12). Then, we may add, shall I judge as I am judged. For judgment is a gift for which God would fit us: insightful, merciful, creative, and utterly true, so different from the mixture of prejudice, anxiety, and ignorant self-assertion that passes for judgment in the absence of anything better. To be equipped to exercise that judgment is to be equipped for the part God has given to mankind in the created order. And now we shall be equipped. For in Jesus Christ exalted and glorified the rule that has been forever God's is also man's. He has opened the Kingdom of Heaven to all believers.

The Opening of the Kingdom   43

Eternal Fire

He has put eternity in man's mind.   ECCLESIASTES 3:11

Whitsunday seems to have drawn the very best out of Bach, and for me it always begins by putting on the turntable the antique Karl Richter recording of the Cantata BWV 34, with its magnificent fugal opening chorus greeting the Holy Spirit: *O ewiges Feuer! O Ursprung der Liebe!* "Eternal fire and wellspring of love!" Entirely in keeping with the Age of Sentiment, you may think, as Bach's libretti always are! Yet that great invocation takes us back behind the subjective enthusiasms of the eighteenth century to the mystery at the heart of the Day of Pentecost itself. Fire eternal! But fire is a happening, not a being; and eternity does not belong to happenings, but to ultimate reality. How can fire be eternal? How can the bush burn, and not be consumed?

We could, of course, say "perennial fire" without raising this question at all. Fire is naturally perennial. Perennially the church finds itself set ablaze by some new movement of revival. Perennially the disciple finds revival touching him or her. Prayer, understanding, ecstasy, fortitude, community, rapture, conscience, boldness of speech: all these and more are given us in special measure from time to time, and we rightly attribute them to God the Spirit. Whenever there is an answer from our side to the invitation from God's side, then we are in the sphere of the Spirit's work. Perennially the Spirit works among us to bring forth our

---

22nd May 1988.

answer. And that is why what we learn about the Holy Spirit in Christian teaching seems both very limited and very expansive. Limited, because our thought passes so quickly over the Spirit himself to the sphere of his working. Expansive, because once we have passed over him there is so much to talk about. The Apostles' Creed is typical: "I believe in the Holy Ghost" we say; and then, immediately, "the holy catholic church, the communion of saints, the forgiveness of sins, the resurrection of the dead and the life everlasting". All of which happen *to us: we* are the church, *we* share the life of saints, *we* have our sins forgiven, *we* shall rise from the dead. These experiences are the answer of our being to what God has given us of his own being in Jesus Christ. We follow Christ, and as we follow, our experience takes these forms: sins forgiven, resurrection, the life of the community. The fire burns, and it burns within us. But is it eternal fire, or merely perennial? When we follow instead the Nicene Creed, we are compelled to pause at this point. We are not allowed to hurry on to one holy catholic and apostolic church, one baptism for the remission of sins, and so on. We have to gaze upon the being of the Spirit himself, "the Lord, the giver of life, who proceeds from the Father; who with the Father and the Son is worshipped and glorified". And then we have to take a breath. This breath forces us to recognise that our perennial answer to God is given us by something prior and greater: God's own eternal answer to God, the divine spirit, the eternal fire.

This truth is very much alive in the minds of our ecumenical discussion-partners in the Eastern Orthodox churches, who struggle faithfully to convict us of what they see as our stubborn Western heresy about the Holy Spirit. In the published records of the Anglican-Orthodox Joint Doctrinal Discussions we find that at one point the Anglican theologians were asked, "In the Anglican view is the revealed glory of God uncreated? If it is, is it the essence of God?" Happily, my learned former Toronto colleague, Professor Eugene Fairweather, was on hand to answer what would for most Anglican theologians have been an incomprehensible question: "It is a revelation of the uncreated through the medium of the created". Which elicited the rejoinder, "Here you follow Augustine!" What matters about that exchange is not whether we do or do not follow Augustine, but whether we have understood the question, which is a question we ought to ask ourselves every

Pentecost. All this religiousness we delight in, ecstatic and formal, individual and corporate, spontaneous and ordered, musical and silent, intellectual and emotional, active and contemplative: is it all *us*, really? Or is it God's own self having dealings with us? To return to Bach, *Wir wünschen, o Höchster, dein Tempel zu sein!* "We want to be a temple for the Most High!" Is the temple inhabited?

I believe we can reach an answer by grasping how Pentecost is new. *I will show wonders in the heavens above and signs on the earth beneath, blood and fire and vapour of smoke. The sun shall be turned to darkness and the moon to blood before the day of the Lord comes, the great and manifest day* (Joel 2:30f.). It is not mere happening and change that fire brings, but disruption. If we think of our experience as merely subject to change and flux, we shall never understand how God can indwell them. Change and flux belong to us, not to God. But if we realise that our human experience can encompass something really new, the thought of divine indwelling opens up to us.

For the new cuts right across our existing framework of human experience. The new defies expectation, extrapolation, prediction, all those laws of change promising a certain stability within the flux of things. And yet it makes sense, not nonsense, of what we have experienced. It is discontinuity, yet it is fulfilment. Not any and every disruption in the course of things counts as something new, only that disruption which takes up the old, broken continuity into itself, and saves it as it destroys it. In the Acts of the Apostles the presence of the Holy Spirit is signalled by miracle. Miracle does not merely defy human expectations; it also satisfies the thread of hope within them. Someone has claimed to have been healed of chronic heart disease at the Diocesan Conference this year. That was miracle. It wouldn't have been a miracle if someone had had a heart attack, however unexpected. Miracle gives fulfilment to hopes lurking within the fabric of experience which have no claims on predictable experience. It is new.

Introduce the new, and you can turn the flux and change of human experience into something we call "history". Time then becomes the stage on which an order emerges from the aimlessness of world events. Consider, for example, one striking historical fact, the emergence of democracy in the West. Forget for a moment the endless corruptions of it, its constant failure to realise itself in actual political structures, the

The Mission of God's Word

dreadful crimes committed or threatened in its name. Forget, too, the formative but inconclusive experiments of the Greek city-states, grounded as they were on the distinction of the free citizen from the slave. And ask, how could it *ever* have seemed possible that menservants and maidservants would prophesy, would contribute to the deliberations of their society, not just as one voice among many, one vote in the ballot box alongside others, but as spokesmen of God, whose voice commands authority and must be heeded? It is a wonderful thing! It springs from that new life in the midst of Western society, the life of Pentecost. For where the new intervenes and reshapes the old, there is God, the Lord and giver of life.

Yet the new is not easy to recognise. Precisely because it *is* new, we have no native capacity to see it, since recognition has to do with the familiar and the old. The new must force itself on us, evoking an act of faith, that is, an experienced discontinuity in our understanding. There is, Christians have dared to claim, one new thing lying at the heart of all new things: that Jesus is Lord. And *nobody can say 'Jesus is Lord' except by the Holy Spirit.*

Pentecost has to be seen, then, not simply as an innovation, but as a reference back to that one decisive innovation, the self-disclosure of God in Jesus Christ. What connects the Spirit of Pentecost to the life, death, and vindication of Jesus?

In the first place we may take the answer of Saint Luke. It is the Ascension of Jesus to the right hand of God, the triumphant coronation of the Son of Man, that forms the basis for this Pentecostal novelty, in which the whole body of disciples is caught up into the triumph. The Acts of the Apostles begins with the Ascension, as St. Luke's Gospel ends with it. The Ascension is the link between then and now. In the Epistle to the Ephesians, too, a verse from Psalm 68 is quoted to make the same link between the Pentecostal experience and Christ: *When he ascended on high, he led a host of captives and gave gifts to men,* the gifts being the manifold gifts of the Spirit. But that by itself does not say enough; for by linking the gift of Pentecost only with that final triumph, of which nothing can be said except that it happened, we effectively sever this life in the Spirit from what can be spoken of in the life of Jesus. And that will lead us down a path which the church later had to condemn under the name of "Montanism", the path of treating the life of

Christ as a mere preliminary to life in the Spirit. So Tertullian argued, disastrously, for innovations in the moral order of the church — the compulsory veiling of virgins, for example, and the prohibition of second marriage after widowhood — on the simple ground that in Jesus' day the time was not ripe for these further disclosures of the will of God. "Righteousness appeared first in rudiments, as natural fear of God; through the law and the prophets it advanced to infancy; through the Gospel to its youth; and now through the Paraclete it is settling into maturity". Newness is then no longer radical newness. It is tamed into a doctrine of progress, a development immanent in the passing of the ages, just as growth is immanent in the newborn baby.

In the second place, then, we may take the answer of Saint Paul. The Spirit, as Christ's Spirit, initiates us into the whole of Christ's life, and especially into his death and resurrection. Again, if followed exclusively, as, say, Bultmann followed it, this approach leads us astray. The actual history of Jesus Christ may be conjured away into a series of mystical laws of spiritual existence, such as that suffering is the true form of victory. There is no longer an achievedness in Christ's work, a finality.

To capture the true relation between the Spirit and Christ we have to sustain a careful balance between the truths in these two approaches. Yes, the Spirit is the sign of Christ's triumph, yet in sharing the Spirit we do not participate only in the triumph, but in the whole of Christ's way, from humility and suffering into the vindication of God. We walk this path after him, and recapitulate it; yet precisely so do we see that he has triumphed and won a company of followers. The gift of the Spirit is, first and foremost, the gift of recapitulating Christ's way; and that recapitulation *is* his triumph and ours, for it establishes his rule in the affairs of the world. He is the radical novelty, the new thing God has done. All things are made new *in him*. The Spirit is God the Recapitulator, who makes the achieved work of Christ present in every age. In recapitulation is our newness. For without God-in-us to answer God-in-Christ we could never answer this newness with a newness of our own.

Can eternity and newness coexist in God? Or, to phrase the question again in terms of the classic controversies of Eastern and Western Christendom, can he who proceeds "from the Father", and so from eternity, be the same as he who proceeds "from the Father and the Son", and so makes all things new? I can only think that since newness trans-

The Mission of God's Word

forms and fulfils the old order, showing us what it was always meant to be, it gives us the clearest grasp of eternity of which we are capable. *He has put eternity in man's mind,* said the preacher, *yet so that he cannot find out what God has done from the beginning to the end,* a text which will serve very well as a meditation for Pentecost. The eternity in man's mind is an empty form, a category of comprehension to which we can give no content, until we grasp the end and purpose of God's doings through this new thing that will complete and fulfil the apparently aimless cycle of world events. But now God has set eternity within our hearts, so that we may confess the end of God's works which he has planned from the beginning. It is the voice of his own Spirit, crying "Jesus is Lord!" It is the fire of his own being attesting the great day of the Lord, when all who call upon his name will be saved.

*   *   *

Open our eyes, o God, that we may see you enthroned on high. Open our ears that we may hear your messengers of peace. Give us the Spirit's voice that we may join the unceasing song of praise, as the hosts of heaven cry "Holy!" And raise us up, that we may ascend upon the ladder joining heaven and earth, even the Son of Man who came down from heaven, Jesus Christ our Lord.

The Community of God's Word

Come!

The Spirit and the bride say,
"Come!" Let him that hears say, "Come!"   REVELATION 22:17

In Holy Scripture we encounter the word "come" commonly enough. The Bible concordance I consulted devotes forty-four columns to it, each of about one hundred entries, and indicates some hundred and twenty different words in Hebrew, Aramaic, Greek, and Latin which the single English word translates. The Old Testament, as you would expect, provides the bulk of these, but my cursory glance turned up only one case where the word "Come!" is used as a kind of prayer in the Old Testament. "Come!" is not something Jewish believers said to God. They said it to one another: *Come, let us return unto the Lord our God!* And God said it to them: *Ho, every one that thirsts, come to the waters!*

But in the New Testament the faithful pray, "Come!" A prayer from the earliest church, preserved in Aramaic in St. Paul, is *Marana-tha,* "Our Lord, come!" And that may strike us as odd. For we could think that the Old Covenant, the time of waiting, would be the time for praying "Come!" and that after the Incarnation, since the anointed one *has* come, there is no further place for praying, "Come!"

Yet "Come!" is the prayer of the church, the prayer of the new times, the prayer to the one who has come. For coming is drawing near; it is an act of affinity, of friendship. And so the coming of God to man as man in

---

23rd December 2003.

Bethlehem opens up the possibility of this prayer. That he *did* come creates the expectation that he *will* come. It is like that with every kind of waiting. Expectancy is predicated on experience. Without the experience we would not know what to expect or why to expect it. Imagine you are waiting for a letter day after day, and say, "How I wish that it would come!" You can only expect it because you have some idea whom it will come from, what it will contain, and why it will be coming at this time. And that idea is formed by what you know already, of the writer, the subject and the circumstances, for otherwise you could not expect anything. So it is with the coming of Christ. The expectancy with which we pray "Come!" springs from his having come. The past event of Christmas forms the horizon of our future. Which is why the Advent season has a double aspect, looking back to Christ's coming to look forward to his coming again.

If we forget that Christ *did* come, our celebration of Christmas is a mere cyclical repetition, a ritual of anticipation and satisfaction which we go through every year in a kind of natural rhythm. When Christmas loses contact with past history, it loses contact with the future, too. Then we do not pray "Come!" except in pretence, as in a children's game where danger and rescue are acted out within a cocoon of familiarity. If, on the other hand, we forget that Christ *will* come, then Christmas is a time of disappointment. As that rather depressive Christmas hymn reminds us:

> Yet with the woes of sin and strife the world has suffered long;
> Beneath the angel-strain have rolled two thousand years of wrong;
> And man at war with man hears not the love-song which
>   they bring:

Which produces a despairing outburst:

> O hush the noise, ye men of strife, and hear the angels sing!

That is produced by an impotent sense of history gone astray, leading nowhere. So Christmas is a time when we need to learn especially to look forward, to pray "Come!"

The Spirit and the bride say, "Come!" It is the prayer of two quite distinct voices.

On the one hand, it is the voice of the Spirit. The one exception to the rule that the Old Testament never prays "Come!" is that passage in which the prophet Ezekiel stands in the valley of dry bones and is told to prophesy, and he prays: *Come from the four winds, o Spirit, and breathe upon these slain that they may live!* And the very same Spirit to whom the prophet cried, *Come from the four winds!* and to whom we pray at Pentecost, *Veni, Creator Spiritus!* now himself cries "Come!" The Spirit's voice speaks from that first God-willed coming, the giving of life which breathed creation into existence and gave each of us our life at the beginning. But now he calls for a completion of that beginning. The Spirit has given life, has given birth to the church in the testimony of Jesus, and now demands fulfilment, the completion of God's purposes for us and for creation.

On the other hand, it is the voice of the bride. Here speaks the church, but not the church as we know it only too well, divided, disorganised, well-meaning, short-sighted, and pompous. Here speaks the community made ready for her divine partner, revealed in a new coherence and maturity. In this prayer we hear the true voice of the church, and it is with that voice that we are invited to join our own: *Let him that hears say, "Come!"* It is not taken for granted that we *do* join our voices to that "Come!" Just because we find ourselves in the church it is not taken as read that we pray that prayer. The question is always asked of us, Are we with the church that prays, "Come!"? Are we among those who hear? Across the divided, disorganised, well-meaning sounds that echo within the church, does *this* voice come across to us as the voice of the Spirit and the bride? For if we hear this prayer, we shall also utter it.

What does it demand of us to utter the prayer, "Come!"?

It demands detachment, and it demands enthusiasm — both together. A detachment, on the one hand, from the great inevitabilities of cosmos and history, among which our life rolls inexorably forward; an enthusiasm, on the other, for the truth of judgment, for hearing the right word spoken. To use the two words that St. John would use at this point: it requires a detachment from the *world,* that system of unchallengeable conditions, that great unarguable framework which lays down terms to us. And it requires an enthusiasm for *life,* which is the possibility that God constantly puts in front of us, life constituted by speaking and acting the truth.

About the days of great distress which were to come upon the earth, Jesus said, *Woe to those who are with child in those days!* And we can add other woes to that. Woe to those who are young in those days! Their enthusiasm for life breeds ambition to accomplish things, and ambition hands them over to the world which lays down its inexorable terms for accomplishment. Woe to those who are old in those days! Their disgust at the world's terms quenches their enthusiasm for life, and hands them over to despair. We need to learn to be old in a young way and young in an old way. We need to pray for irony, seeing through the dangers of our years and cherishing detachment and enthusiasm.

The focal point at which the prayer "Come!" will be demanded of us is the point of death. For here everything we have done in life is tested. Here it becomes plain whether we have learned to love life rightly, so as to look still more eagerly for a different life. One of the most beautiful of Bach's Motets, written, it is supposed, for a funeral, has the title "Komm! Jesu, komm!". How striking that our ancestors thought a funeral an occasion for mourners to rehearse the attitude appropriate to their own deaths! They were concerned less to comfort those who had lost the dead than to comfort those who must themselves prepare to die. It is as though the voice of the Christian dead themselves counsels us as we stand at the graveside. Three stark opening chords set the word "Komm!" three times, and then break into a strong forward-moving triple rhythm, leaving us in no doubt that this is a prayer empowered by hope, not victim to resignation. The dying Christian who sings "World, goodnight!" does so only in order to claim another world, the world of the resurrection, of Jesus Christ himself, the Way, the Truth, and the Life, who is even now *coming*. The prayer of the prophet in the face of death, *Come from the four winds, o Spirit, and breathe upon these slain!* is turned in the Spirit's own voice to a personal cry to the risen Jesus: *Even so come, Lord Jesus!*

But what needs to be on our lips supremely at the hour of death needs to be our prayer at every point in life. "Come!" is a prayer for a new world, and it constantly strains to see the anticipations of that new world given us in this one. It sets a bridle on our ambition, which would sell us bound and gagged to this world, and it carries our steps up out of the sump of despair, into which this world would bring us.

We must pray "Come!" over all our work, that often dangerously satisfying and often dangerously despairing engagement with the world. All our work, from planning a meeting to drawing up accounts, from the answering of e-mails to George Herbert's famous sweeping of a room, is a moment at which we can pray to see Jesus come to us. But let us take a noble work as an example, since it is with the noble and fulfilling that we think we can dispense with praying "Come!" What does it mean, for example, to call upon him to come as we write a sermon? Or listen to one, for that matter, since a sermon is hardly less hard work to listen to than to write? The writing of a sermon is the making of an artefact, like any other artefact; the hearing of a sermon is an act of attention, like any other attention; and in worldly terms either may be done well or badly, the sermon exquisitely or clumsily composed, the attention acute or flagging. In the end we may doubt whether it makes much difference. But when we pray "Come!" something else may occur, something that takes us beyond the thing done or made well or badly. A fire from heaven may descend to devour the sacrifice, opening up a communication of life such as cannot be accounted for by what we do, a passage from our work into the life of the resurrection.

We must pray "Come!" over all our anxieties. Perhaps as we wait for that letter to arrive day by day, we are held up, as it seems, because our attention is so focussed on it. To pray for that other coming is to be freed from dependence upon this one, however important to our life in the world it may be. And so it is to be free from what has come to constitute the world for us, to lay down terms to us. We call Jesus to our side, and he puts that other coming in its proper place.

We must pray "Come!" over all our failures. Our sense of being defeated, ashamed before the demands of life is the vice-like grip by which the world imposes its terms upon us. The mutual disappointment in which we fail to be what we might have been to others, or they to us, is overtaken as Jesus comes to us, allows us to walk free of the world's terms and their shame, forms us into what we are given to be for him, and so also for others.

We must pray "Come!", finally, over all our rest: over our holidays, over our retirement. For rest from labour is vacancy and emptiness, unless it is shaped and enlivened by vital expectation. Jesus comes to us, and we look forward, not just to more of the same, more labour, more rest, but to another life, and to one who fills our future with his presence.

To help us learn to pray this one-word prayer in every circumstance of life, we are given two other brief words in the passage read to us this morning. They keep our one word in its place; they give it its context and its point.

Let him that thirsts come! As we pray "come!" we ourselves come. We come to quench our thirst with the waters of life. Prayer is as such an answer to the invitation given from the other side: *Ho, every one that thirsts, come to the waters!* To pray "come!" is to take of the waters of life that are given us now, to anticipate the waters of life that are to be given to us later.

There is also a sequel to our prayer, a positive answer to it, given to us even before the prayer is uttered: *Yes, I come quickly!* That is a promise for all our days and for the day of our death, which opens its horizon beyond our days and beyond the days of this world's history. Jesus has promised, *I come!*

Left Behind in the Place

This is why I left you in Crete.   TITUS 1:5

The new Bishop of Knaresborough, in a farewell column in the Oxford Diocesan newspaper, reminded his friends that he first came to Oxford with a Partnership in Mission team that visited the diocese fifteen years ago; and was, as it were, left behind, to discharge the duties of Archdeacon and Canon for a while. But always, he insisted, remaining, as he began, a partner in mission. I shall miss that partnership. My family arrived in Oxford just a few months ahead of the Westons; so you will allow me the feeling, perhaps, that in heading off to other partnerships just as we were settling into our stride, he has shown himself of a hasty and restless disposition. But what else would you look for from a partner in *mission?* Mission is footloose; mission is mobile; mission has the horizon in its view. It is carried forward by the Spirit of God from Jerusalem to Samaria to Macedonia to Rome, and on to the ends of the earth.

Yet, on its swirling, restless way, it leaves one or another of us off, to stay for a while, here or there. I was reminded of Saint Paul writing to Titus: *This is why I left you in Crete.* Left behind at Gortyn, the island's capital — I had to look up the name, it had slipped my mind — while Paul and his team pressed forward to preach the gospel somewhere else,

---

3rd December 1997 in York Minister, at the consecration of the Rt. Rev. Frank Weston, Archdeacon of Oxford, as Bishop of Knaresborough.

St. Titus became, with St. Timothy, the role model left by the apostolic church for the office of the bishop as it was later to develop. Left behind, not to settle down and become sedentary, but to hasten the movement of mission onward. For the Spirit of God, whose mission it is, is no mere *traveller,* like those who pound up and down the A1 without a thought for the towns and villages whose names appear on road signs as they speed by. The Spirit moves *through* our communities, not *past* them. He carries them with him on his way. He claims their partnership in mission; he mobilises them as he moves. And he leaves this person or that at Gortyn or at Knaresborough, so that neither Gortyn nor Knaresborough should be left out of his great progress.

The church's ancient habit of naming bishops after places — a habit we are so attached to that a Suffragan Bishop, too, must be assigned a place — is meant to lead us to the heart of this dialectical logic about places and movement. Often enough the church has missed the point of it. It has treated the place-name as an excuse to be sedentary. In the days of Saint Wilfred there were missionaries in Yorkshire; but now, we think, we have bishops instead, who are features of the social landscape, grand and dilapidated like the landed gentry, and, like them, rooted to the spot. But if we think so, we have not understood how places enter the missionary economy of the Spirit. A place is a social phenomenon; it has the mobility of those who people it; it is not a space "in which" so much as a space "to which" and "from which". The place where the Holy Spirit extends his mission has people flowing into it. Places emerge out of mere spaces as people gather, to seek the relief of their needs, the renewal of their lives, the advance of their concerns, and to hear and invoke the name of Jesus, whom God has set forward as an ensign to the peoples. So mission penetrates *inwards* within a place; it gives the place its centre by the proclamation of the word of life and the celebration of the sacraments. The geography of Europe bears constant witness in its place-names to the work of mission that has formed its points of gathering out of mere space. As the mission of the Spirit goes forward, the identity of the place becomes defined, its common life structured and beautified, its people's energies released to the service of God's love and the learning of God's truth.

Yet together with this inward penetration of the place, mission reaches out beyond its frontiers. As the life of a place is deepened, struc-

The Community of God's Word

tured, and beautified, so it must look out to another place, a place not yet so defined and structured and beautified. Only by reaching out to the *other* place can *this* place avoid the fate of collapsing inwards with its own self-absorption.

And here is the logic of that threefold order of ministry which serves the people of God in their witness and worship. If the deacon is to give structure to the Christian life of a place, if the priest is to maintain its responsibility to the gospel word and sacrament, the bishop is to keep it looking out beyond its borders. When Knaresborough is given a Rector, it is given someone to secure the roots of its life in the proclamation of the word and celebration of the sacraments. And it wants its Rector right there, on the spot. When Knaresborough is given a Bishop, it is given someone to safeguard the spiritual highways which link its life with the life of Leeds and Ripon and Richmond. It does not want him right there; it does not even mind if he lives in Leeds, because it wants him out and about, moving around between itself and others.

Where episcopal ministry is strong and effective, we see much contact taking place. Christian people here are engaged with Christian people there. When we receive the Bishop in our place, we receive an invitation not to let ourselves become an isolated, self-sufficient place, but to find ourselves in missionary cooperation with other places. *We ought to receive such people,* St. John tells us, *that we may be cooperators in the truth* (3 John 8). He is the minister of the church's cooperation: telling Chapeltown how it can help Hawes, telling Hawes what it has got that Harrogate could use, telling Harrogate how it can strengthen life in Reeth. And by the same principle he is the link with other bishops and with other groups of places where the name of Jesus is confessed. He is the minister of the church's unity, the representative of one to another.

Receive one another, St. Paul tells us, *as Christ received you* (Rom. 15:7). Through the Bishop we receive those whom we cannot receive in person; through the Bishop we know ourselves received by them. When he comes to lay hands on new Christians who confess their faith in Richmond, his prayers sum up not only the prayers of parents and godparents and fellow-believers in North Yorkshire, but the prayers of city congregations in Nairobi, the prayers of small town congregations in Ontario, the prayers of our Porvoo partners in Iceland, the prayers of the Saints and Martyrs of Asia, prayers made in Japanese, in Spanish, in Russian, and in a thousand other tongues. Through the Bishop we learn to listen to a church that worships on every line of longitude and latitude and in every conceivable variety of human circumstance. A church that through his ministry receives us as Christ has received us, a church of those we may receive in turn as Christ has received them.

And there are other Christians, again, on whose behalf the Bishop comes to us. They are the Christian of past generations, who share with us in the communion of saints. They have given their lives to the witness and service of the gospel, and we are the unknown answers to their prayers. To them we have obligations of loyalty — which does not mean slavish imitation, for they were not slavishly imitative, but creative and inventive; but it does mean fidelity to the same gospel that they believed, a readiness to learn from their witness. The Bishop of Knaresborough has engraved on his pectoral cross words from a typically powerful clausula of Saint Augustine of Hippo, *Omnes amandi,* "All must be loved!" The sentence is fine, but so is the source. It is right that *that* voice, too, from ancient Roman Africa should be heard in a Bishop's ministry in Yorkshire along with many other voices of other Christians for whom he speaks to us. If the *vertical* rule of our lived faith is, and must always be, the rule of the word of Christ, given through the testimony of prophets, apostles, and evangelists to which nothing can be added; yet the *horizontal* rule must be the voice of other Christians, and not only Christians of our times but of times past to us, though to God they are always present. The Bishop's role is to recall us to tradition — not to immobility, but to living continuity with what we have received and those from whom we have received it. Ages and periods in the church's life, like individuals and communities, can never live alone; they are most truly themselves when they are in company with others. To close off our place against other places is to make our place sterile. So it is, too, if we close off our time, and look on other times with a parochial suspicion and contempt.

The Bishop serves the church's mission; he serves its unity; he serves its tradition. And all these aspects of his service converge on a single theological moment, a point in the proclamation of the gospel which it is especially the bishop's office to uphold: he serves the coming of the Kingdom of God.

It is a good thing to consecrate a Bishop in Advent and send him off on his diocesan tasks in Epiphany. For he can go with the Advent proclamation in his ears, *Behold, the Bridegroom! Come out to meet him!* (Matt. 25:6). The bishop, too, is always *coming,* never simply *there.* But he is not the coming bridegroom. He is a continuing forerunner, a John the Baptist who will call people out to meet him. And he can hear the promise of Epiphany, which follows from the Advent message directly: *a light to lighten the nations, and to be the glory of the whole earth.* The Bishop comes to open the windows of our place, so we may look out on the nations and see the brightness of Christ's glory shed over the widest imaginable landscape. In Advent we remember that every loyalty, every focus of identity, every bond of obligation, not least our local loyalties to homes and towns, must be dissolved before the one loyalty, the obligation to the coming Kingdom. *Owe no man anything,* we hear on Advent Sunday, *except to love one another* (Rom. 13:8). *Omnes amandi!* In Epiphany we find we have not lost or abandoned our loyalties and identities, but they have been taken up within this new and vast identity, the Kingdom which brings *every nation, from all tribes and peoples and tongues* (Rev. 7:9) to be represented before the throne. We find them there again with new breadth, new neighbourhood, new communications, new partnerships, a new and universal dignity.

On my one visit to Crete many years ago I tried to visit the site of ancient Gortyn, just to see where it was that St. Paul left St. Titus to become the role model of a bishop. It was one of those tourist visits that went wrong. The remains of the acropolis and of the Haghios Titos basilica, which the guidebooks assured me were to be admired, remained stubbornly out of sight as I stood where the bus set me down, peering round at the olive-groves. Well, there was a fitness about that, too. *Titus,* I could have read in the second Epistle to Timothy, *has gone to Dalmatia.* He had fulfilled his mission and gone on; centuries later the whole place had fulfilled its mission and gone on. The evidence for its effectiveness lay all around in the still living Christian life of Crete. Then, as it were, it left a clearing behind it, a space for the coming kingdom to enter, and surrendered its identity for safekeeping to one who will never let its name slip his mind. I shall view Gortyn on the last day, I trust, in its Christians who stand before the throne of grace, stronger and more independent-minded for having been well bishoped. And today we pray: May they find their equals in the Christians of North Yorkshire!

Dividing the Kingdom

This altar shall be split asunder.   I KINGS 13:3

I have resolved to exercise an evangelical liberty this morning and break with the prescribed readings to discuss a strange, rather forbidding story from the Book of Kings. I do this because I think we ought to consider the threat of disunity that hangs over the worldwide Anglican churches at this moment as the Archbishops gather at Lambeth, and this story is a focus around which I have tried to think about our responsibilities.

It is a story about two temptations of a prophet, a servant of the word of God. The only thing we need to know about its two principal characters is that they *are* prophets. They have no names. But the story has a setting in the history of a nation. The schismatic King Jeroboam, who founded the separate Northern kingdom of Israel by leading the Northern tribes in rebellion against King David's grandson, was to receive a message from God. To deliver it a prophet from the Southern kingdom of Judah was sent North to Samaria, across the newly created border, to say "No!" to the division of the kingdom. Jeroboam would not establish a stable political entity. The altar on which he sacrificed would be split asunder, like the kingdom he himself had divided in two.

12th October 2003, responding to the first wave of the crisis in the Anglican Communion caused by the election of the Rt. Rev. Gene Robinson as Bishop of New Hampshire. He was consecrated in November 2003.

The Community of God's Word

The angry king attempted to arrest the intruder, but there followed a chilling miracle: the royal hand stretched out in command was withered. Then, at the prophet's word, it was restored. So the frightened monarch changed his manner: the prophet was urged to dine as the royal guest and accept rewards. And this was the first of his two temptations.

He met it splendidly. *I will eat and drink nothing in this place, for the Lord's command to me was to eat and drink nothing, and not to go back by the way I came!*

The servant of God's word must be the servant of the word only, beholden to nothing and no one else. Kings recruit the power of others to serve the interests of their kingdom. But the servant of the word is not to be recruited. He doesn't have God's approval at his command to bargain with. God's word is not an asset, to purchase a secure place in the world; it is a charge to deliver, and then he is to absent himself.

It is easy to misunderstand this. It is not that the word of God is indifferent to the needs of governments and societies. It is not that it is always critical, never constructive. It is simply that it is sovereign. It will not be negotiated with. It will shed the light of its truth uncompromisingly, whether to be acted on or ignored. So the messenger is at its disposal, coming and going as it bids. The servant of the word must be free with the freedom of the word.

Now we come to the second temptation. Among those who observed the encounter between prophet and king there were some who were deeply in sympathy with the visitor. One of these was an old man, also a prophet, who felt a deep longing. Fellowship, communion of spirit, open confidence with an equal who had performed his task and conquered his temptation, relief from the terrible burden of loneliness that all who serve God's word must sometimes bear: that longing was his temptation, and he yielded to it. He saddled his ass and rode to intercept the other on his way home. *I also am a prophet, and an angel commanded me to bring you home with me to eat and drink!* Did he know that he was lying? Or was he even deceived by his own emotional need? It does not matter. For the Southerner was not on his guard. He, too, was lonely, emotionally drained by his confrontation. Longing heart spoke to longing heart. So taking this word as God's, which it was not, he turned from the path God had set for him, and went to the old man's home.

It is easy, again, to misunderstand. It is not that we are *not* called to fellowship. It is not that the true of heart can never share together, plan together, strengthen one another. Bleak indeed would the world be if God were never in the midst when two or three were gathered together. In fact, we are always together: Jesus has founded his church, he has poured out his Spirit upon it, he has given it its sacraments of baptism and eucharist. But the church formed by God's word cannot produce its *own* word of comfort, it cannot console and strengthen itself. The church finds its fellowship only as each member listens to God's speech. Then it finds that it is already together, a community of listening.

The story unfolds in tragedy. Where the false word had prevailed, the true word asserted itself. Judgment was spoken to the Southern prophet *while they were seated at table,* and through the very one who had led him astray. *You have defied the word of the Lord! Your body shall not be laid in the grave of your forefathers!* Anxiously, hastily, the moment of communion shockingly interrupted, the journeying prophet makes his farewells; and then, as he travels, a lion falls on him and kills him. But tragedy is not the last word. Reports reach Samaria of a strange phenomenon, and the old man goes to investigate. There on the road stands the prophet's ass, keeping watch where his master's body lies, neck broken but otherwise unharmed, while the lion stands by it, neither mauling the body nor attacking the ass. It is a sign from God, the old man judges — a true prophet now! — that what the dead man spoke against Jeroboam's kingdom shall not fail. He takes his friend's body home with him for burial and mourning, and the tomb is still to be seen there when, centuries later, conquering King Josiah reaches Samaria from Jerusalem.

There is, I think, no more telling image of the church and of its always so compromised witness, than that solemn tableau of the disgraced prophet, slain but not consumed, watched over by the ass and by the lion. Not even the prophet's failure can suppress the voice of God as he speaks to rebuke and recall, to challenge and forgive. So let us pursue the implications for the life of our church, called to be a prophetic church, serving the word of God.

It faces two temptations. The first is the world; the second, and more difficult, is the church itself. For the church of Jesus Christ can only be itself when wholly engaged upon mission, the mission of God's word. There is a paradox in what theologians call "ecclesiology", the doctrine of the church. The church is what we are called to *be;* and if we are busy being the church, we do not have an objective point of view from which to examine the church and talk about it. While if we are *not* busy being the church, we are not in a position to examine it and talk about it. Someone drew my attention the other day to the fact that the church is hardly mentioned in the course of Morning Prayer. Everything in that liturgy expresses the church, yet only at two points does the church actually surface. One is in the *Te Deum,* where "the holy church throughout all the world doth acknowledge thee . . .", and the other is in the creed: "I believe in the Holy Ghost, the holy catholic church. . . ." When we look back at how our hymn of praise arose, and see ourselves in the succession of apostles, prophets, and martyrs, when we recount in gratitude and faith what God has done for us, then we understand ourselves as the church of Jesus Christ. We know that he has provided us with fellowship in his service, reaching back over the centuries to the eyewitness generation. He has given us his Spirit, all the strengthening and consolation that we need. And we stray from this when we put the church at the centre, when we cease to press towards the goal of knowing Christ and making him known, and aim instead at getting the church right — being its minders, keepers, strategists, reformers. We have our plans to purify it, reorganise it, modernise it, redefine it so that you can see at a glance who belongs and who doesn't. Busying ourselves about the church, we shield ourselves from the word that has to be discerned, proclaimed, and lived. We parade as problem-solvers, when we ought to hear and obey.

Let me mention another story from the Old Testament, shorter but no less forbidding. It is set a century or so before Jeroboam of Samaria, at the beginning of the reign of David. The ark of the covenant, that empty wooden chest that symbolised God's presence in his community, had for years been kept in a rural shrine, but was now to be brought into the citadel of David's newly conquered capital, Jerusalem. The procession comprised a mighty military escort, two priests from the rural shrine in the place of honour beside the ox-drawn cart which bore the ark, and dancers and musicians leading the way. Then at a critical moment the oxen stumbled. The cart tilted. The ark, unstable, slid. And one of the priests, called Uzzah, grasped the ark to steady it with his hand, and immediately fell dead.

We may well find this very upsetting. David did. He left the ark right there in a farmhouse where the accident happened, and stormed off in a rage. His plans to bring the ark to the city were shelved. If it was going to be that touchy, it had better not be there at all! But there was a lesson the king had to learn. What Uzzah the priest had done was precisely what David wanted to do: to assert proprietorship, to be the guardian and protector of God. But nobody protects God. To assume this tutelary posture is to lay unholy hands upon the holy. David had to learn a different way of relating to the one who protected him.

When the thunderclouds began to form over our Anglican communion of churches a year or more ago, there were many Uzzahs. Hands darted out from all sides to grab the church, to set it on its proper footing, to stop it falling this way or that. We have yet to learn what David had to learn. So I have no project today for *rescuing* the church. It is enough that we should *be* the church as we are bidden, recognise God in our midst, go on our mission at the behest of God's word, not eat and drink on the way, and not return by the way we came. And while we devote ourselves to *that,* the safety of the church can be left where responsibility for it belongs.

The extraordinary meeting of the Primates will gather at Lambeth next week to address the problems created for the communion by the decisions of the General Convention of the Episcopal Church of the USA. If we think we love the church, we shall pray for that meeting. For our Primates will be confronted not by one but two temptations. One will be the temptation of the world, and some of them, no doubt, will find it attractive. They will want the church to accommodate to the realities of late modern life. They will want to negotiate an unexposed position for the church in a context of changing public norms. They will want to exchange the role of prophets for the role of managing directors.

Others will resist this temptation, and on them, perhaps, the worse and more difficult temptation will press: to secure the church by dividing the kingdom. Someone is likely to suggest that two churches of likeminded believers will be happier and cosier than one church discordant: why should not those who care for the church's integrity gather round a single table to eat and drink, and why should others not find it convenient to let them? This offers peace, or seems to. But its real appeal is the offer of relief — relief from anger, relief from struggle, a space for consolation. An attractive prospect! But not what our baptismal vows promised.

God sent his prophet northwards to say "No!" to the division of the kingdom. The word of God will maintain its right to the whole, and so must we. That means a constant, insistent searching of the word, sharing of the word, proclaiming of the word, re-discovering of the word. I don't say that the way of the word is easy, or will quickly yield agreement on the matters that currently divide us. I do say — and this may surprise you — that the way of the word has not yet been tried. But suppose it had been ventured a thousand times and a thousand times failed, the old positions entrenched yet deeper? Then we would have to try it once more, still patiently, still searchingly, until God was ready to act. For the way of the word is God's only way.

The way of dividing the kingdom is no way at all. The unity it offers is not unity in *truth,* for it is a compromise based on *not* speaking the truth to one another. And it is not the way of purity, either; for a church locked out from its mission field, refusing the call to service of the word, would need to establish its own purity by a zeal for exclusion. Its fate would be that of all such sectarian movements, to consume itself in a competition for rigour. To an altar raised in such a way and for such a purpose God's word is implacable: *This altar shall be split asunder!*

Centuries after the unhappy prophet travelled north along the road from Judah to Samaria, God sent another prophet on that same journey into that same hill-country where Jeroboam once built his altar. This prophet was sent not to say "No!", but to say "Yes!" He did not refuse food and drink, but asked for a cup of water. *What! you a Jew ask a drink of me, a Samaritan?* — for Jeroboam's border endured in people's minds. *If only you knew what God gives,* he replied, *and who it is that asks you for a drink, you would ask him and he would give you living water.* Jesus' "Yes" presupposed the earlier prophet's "No". "No" to the division of the kingdom promised and "Yes" to reunite it. And in that "Yes" the word of God was wholly and unchallengeably sovereign, and around it there arose a new community of belief and joy: *When the Samaritans came to him, they pressed him to stay with them; and he stayed there two days* (John 4:40).

Reading

His delight is in the law of the Lord ...   PSALM I:2

Tuesday mornings my wife used to leave early for her class; and we explained to our infant son that she was teaching the young men and women to read their books. It seemed to satisfy him — offering, no doubt, some reassurance that if she and I should ever tire of *The Story of Babar,* there would be trained personnel to assume our office. I sometimes wondered what the young men and women would think of this description of their studies; but I hoped they would recognise it as the best account of a University Arts course that could be found. The second week in Advent, with its prayer that we may "read, mark, learn and inwardly digest", usually coincides in this University with Admissions Week, when tutors try to find the students, and students the tutors, with whom they may hope to get along comfortably for three years. One could simplify those interviews, so trying to both parties, by cutting them down to one question: Can you read?

We think we do it, but mostly we don't. To read is to get inside another person's mind, to think with another person's thoughts, to grasp the world as another person grasps it. If we don't know how to do that, we can never get in touch with people who have lived at different periods and in different circumstances from our own. And in that case we are imprisoned in the narrow range of our own direct experience or in

4th December 1988.

the stifling cultural perspectives of our own class, nation, or period of history. Reading is the key that lets us out of prison into a broad landscape where we may walk up and down and learn things that no living person can teach us.

At a certain point in Israel's history, somewhere about the late seventh century BC, scribes and prophets were swept off their feet by a sudden discovery of the importance of reading. This was the so-called "Deuteronomistic" age, and it left a considerable fallout in the Old Testament scriptures. Here is an instance, the first verse of the first Psalm: *Blessed is the man who walks not in the counsel of the wicked, nor stands in the way of sinners, nor sits in the seat of scoffers; but his delight is in the law of the Lord, and on his law he meditates day and night.* A twice-daily discipline of attention to a text, probably by recitation, will shape the career of the one who is counted happy. The poet delicately makes the contrast between the way this person is open to influence and the way that others are open to influence. They *walk in the counsel of the wicked;* they *stand in the way of sinners;* they *sit in the seat of scoffers.* They begin with the practical advice they receive from those who seem to know their way around; they conform to all the current practices; they take over the common judgments which society passes upon those it does not understand. These three phrases lead us from an air of business — they *walk* — to a static negativity of mind — they *sit.* By contrast, the Reading Man (as we may call him or her) begins from a strange stillness, *like a tree* — not a dynamic image! — *planted by streams of water which yields its fruit in its season, and its leaf does not wither. In all that he does he prospers.* From the apparently motionless attention to what lies outside his own sphere of action, drawing on life-sources not of his own self-generated energy, he turns out to be an effective actor, producing results that have real life and do others real good. The paradox of the Reading Man is that this rootedness is essential to life and activity.

But, of course, the contrast is not only between how the two types of person open themselves to influence, but between the different influences to which each is open. A paean in praise of reading is, perhaps, still acceptable in our age — though each new generation brought up on the manipulative skills of Information Technology finds the spiritual discipline harder to acquire. But here is a suggestion that goes further, a suggestion that it matters *what* one reads. Do we detect the clammy hand of censorship? Can it matter what one reads, so long as one reads something? Yes, it can. The mature man or woman will read anything, it is true, but will demonstrate discrimination in what he or she reads with most persistence and delight. It matters what frames of understanding we construct to interpret the world by. Some books develop some interpretative tendencies, some others. If you meet someone who, on first acquaintance, shows a deep and discerning appreciation of the art of Jane Austen, you will know that there is someone you could trust your children to — though also, probably, someone who would be cautious about accepting the responsibility for them! On the other hand, when Mary Shelley wants to convey what sort of figure Frankenstein's monster will turn out to be, she has him teach himself to read on Plutarch's *Lives,* Milton's *Paradise Lost,* and Goethe's *Sorrows of Werther.*

But *his delight is in the law of the Lord.* That says something more than that he reads *good* books! It refers to a *canonical* text, normative and central, guiding one's reading of all other texts, a Holy Scripture which (in whatever way) God has "caused to be written" for our instruction. What are we to make of this idea? I can neither explore it nor defend it at any length. I can only point out two conditions for its intelligibility. In the first place, the idea of a central, normative text corresponds to the idea of a central, normative strand in history. Is there, as it were, a heartbeat from which the whole vitality and growth of history is sustained? The privileged book must be witness to privileged events. Recognising such events requires faith — not in opposition to reason, but as a foundational moment in the exercise of reason, the moment of recognition that singles out and identifies the hermeneutic centre. If, then, there is a canonical text, there is also a kind of reading that corresponds to it — not an absolutely different kind of reading from that with which we attend to other texts, but a heightened, focussed form of it, a reading done with faith.

In the second place a central, normative text will open up other texts, not close them off. It will be known, in fact, precisely by the light it sheds, making the obscure and illegible clear and intelligible. In the dark ages it was a natural expression of Christian faith that the study of the Scriptures in the monasteries led to the preservation of classical literature; and it was a natural expression of Christian faith in the middle ages that the study of the Scripture in the Universities accompanied the development of an Arts education. But the central text can shed its light for us only if we are prepared for it to do so. That is to say, we must *want* a single source of light to illumine the wide variety of texts that we may read and to help us read them with consistency and integrity. If we are charmed by the idea that some hidden and secreted text may offer us a hiding-hole away from the light, if we hedge our bets to provide ourselves with an alternative standpoint, if we hope to evade ourselves and our commitments, to escape our world and its history, by reading ourselves into another, then we shall have no use for a canonical text. For if there is a canonical text, there must be the reading that corresponds to it, a reading done with faith *and love.* Faith identifies the centre, love reaches out from the centre to touch the perimeter. Saint Augustine was not wrong to think that at the centre of the centre (as it were), at the core of the core-text, lay the law of love. From that point all roads lie open. "Here is our ethics, our logic, our physics!" he declared. Here, too, are our history and our social theory. Here is our access to reading the world the way it is.

The canonical text stands in a privileged place at the heart of the Christian liturgy. It is a warning at the centre of religious practice against a very characteristic religious mistake. Religious people feel. They feel the unity of the soul with God; they feel it to the point where the whole world around them seems to collapse into the self, swallowed up in a vortex of religious sensibility. They are touched by God within themselves, and they know that they are enhanced. But the speech about God which issues from this encounter is all divine energy without divine perception; so taken by itself, it lies. In the view of Nietzsche Christianity as a whole was no more than a timid version of this heightened religious feeling. "Surprised and stupefied . . . by the beam of divine mercy . . . man gave vent to a cry of rapture and for a moment believed that he bore all heaven within him. It is upon this pathological excess of feeling that all the psychological sensations of Christianity operate; it desired to destroy, shatter, stupefy, intoxicate". What Nietzsche did not recognise was another, quite different beam of mercy, shining not on the soul from the heaven within it, but on the world from the heaven within the world: a word of mercy issuing from the empty tomb of Christ and taking form as a gospel.

Catholic (small "c") Christianity proves itself against much delusive enthusiasm by the spiritual exercise which perfectly responds to the gospel, which is reading. No spiritual discipline, not even prayer itself, is so important to it. Catholic Christianity has, of course, its moments of prophesying. It has its pulpit. But at the heart of its worship is not the pulpit but the lectern. Reading is the act that opens us to the voice of Jesus' witnesses, and so opens us to history, to the world, and to the empty tomb at the world's centre. It requires a spiritual self-giving and flexibility, an emptying of our own self-imagined visions in order to be filled with others' testimony.

But precisely that which is so important and so easily lost in the church is most important, and most easily lost, in the University. The great figures in academic life are not those who write big books, but who read well; and they are surprisingly rare. Or perhaps not surprisingly, since the emptying of self which reading requires is alien to the academic mind as well, full as it is of wonderfully interesting thoughts that demand early publication, clever responses, and retorts that prove a book worthless before one has got to the end of it. Here, too, the stillness necessary to hear what is meant is hard to achieve. Those who have this great virtue are peculiarly luminous; they ennoble the lives of others by emancipating others from the prisons of fashionable thinking. Invariably they are storm-beaten individuals, since they do not consent to the fashionable put-downs which constitute the meat and drink of academic debate. They resist fashion, which fashion never likes, not with the posturing resistance of counter-suggestibility, which is not independence, merely a negative echo, but with the rooted firmness of an acquired perspective. At the end of 1988 I salute two such figures who touched my life, and who died this year. They are the American theologian Paul Ramsey of Princeton and the Canadian George Grant of Halifax. Reading men, both of them. And in either case their reading was founded in a commitment to read in the law of the Lord. When I contemplate the extraordinary potency of their lives, what can I do but agree with the Psalmist that they were, indeed, blessed?

The Community of God's Word

Asking

Ask and it will be given you. LUKE 11:9

I have an affinity with Rogation Sunday, "Asking Sunday". The first sermon I preached as a Canon of Christ Church was at Rogation Sunday Matins, since when it has fallen to my lot quite frequently (something, perhaps, to do with the Precentor's computer), so as to spin one of those threads that serve to unify one's life. And here I am in this pulpit again, trying to encourage you once again to ask God for things. I feel close to Jesus' message when I do this, and I seem to understand how difficult his task was. I could enthuse you much more quickly (for I know you well enough to know this much) with a sermon on the doctrine of the Trinity. A self-sufficient, self-directive, highly reflective, altogether *adult* congregation does not take naturally to being told, *Ask and it will be given you.* Of course, as a matter of daily reality, we do ask, perpetually. A growing sector of the population seems to make the filling in of grant applications more or less its sole means of earning a livelihood. But it is strictly non-religious, all this asking that we do. And the reason for that is that it is surrounded in our minds with a sense of shame. The very mention in polite society of a grant application can be counted on

---

21st May 1995. The financial crisis referred to had arisen from some bad investment decisions by the Church Commissioners which came to public notice earlier in the year.

to provoke an embarrassed giggle, as though one had mentioned something risqué.

When we ask, we reveal the content of our wills. They are disclosed to the scrutiny of God, and to our own scrutiny; and our self-image takes an awful knock. Our wills are not naked and clean and upright and heroic. They are bent double, entangled, enmired in the petty and the routine. What we want, we discover, is a miserable pay rise to put us on an equal footing with our colleague at work; we want fine weather on Thursday for our half day off; we want the children to come home from school in a decent temper and to do their homework without fuss; we want some medicine that will settle our bowel disorder; we want a good review for our article, even if it does have its weaknesses. Trite, all of them, and they make us thoroughly ashamed. If we were not told to ask for them, we should never have to face the fact that we wanted them. They would simply take the form of vaguely diffused anxiety, the causes of which could be left to the imagination. As we all know, the anxious mien and the shortish temper can, in the right proportions, cut quite a dash and make us seem interesting and important people. Asking involves a degrading self-knowledge; it is very much like confessing sin.

Again, in asking we reveal our dependence. Some of us have difficulty even asking for directions in a strange town because it exposes our position as inexperienced and vulnerable. When we ask, we confess that something lies outside our power; even if it lies within our power, it lies outside our power to ensure that we achieve the good we hope to gain by it. Our wills, for all their resolution, their persistence, their strength of decision, are inadequate to carry us where we strive to go.

And so at the very heart of Jesus' message is the simple demand, *Ask and it will be given you*. Perhaps everything else in the gospel is there by implication: repentance, faith, good works, the promise of salvation. Only ask. And this most simple of commands is the most difficult to accept. The theologian in us heaps up doubts. Is it not preposterous to try to interest the universal God in our own petty wants? And given he is interested, is it not lacking in faith to try to hold his interest, or increase it? The pragmatist in us resists the idea of handing over responsibility for what we should be doing ourselves. There is a prayer — and I beg your pardon if it is a favourite of yours, for I know it has its admirers — which runs, "Give us grace to accept with serenity the things that cannot be changed, courage to change the things that should be changed, and the wisdom to distinguish". It doesn't see any need to ask for grace to ask. The world's agenda divides into things that lie within our power, for which we take responsibility, and things that lie outside our power, about which there is nothing to be done. God give us grace to realise that if we don't do something, nobody does! That is a monomaniac's prayer! And of course, with such an outlook life becomes a gloomy business indeed! Nothing to make, nothing to appreciate, nothing to enjoy, nothing to recount, nothing to sanctify, nothing to celebrate, just an endless string of deplorable circumstances, to be changed or else put up with!

We are commanded to ask. Rogation Sunday lies between Easter and Ascension. To live the Easter life with the risen Lord is to learn joy, the disposition of the affections which triumphs over the anxiety and dread cast by the shadow of death. The Collect for the Fourth Sunday after Easter spoke of God's power to "order the unruly wills and affections of sinful men". When he calls us to ask, God accepts our wills and affections. They may seem mean to us, but they are not too mean for him. He would rather have us stand before him willing and desiring than purged, as some misguided mystics have recommended, of all desire. He will not pour out our purposes upon the ground merely because they are base purposes. He will redeem them, not redeem us from them. But this he does by setting them a new goal, a new object of ultimate desire. The Kingdom of Heaven, the manifest rule of God in Christ, fleetingly seen through the clouds that hid the Lord from his disciples' eyes on the Mount of Olives — that is something worth desiring! And to desire that, we must learn to desire other things *for* that. Only if we ask for them can we be taught to ask for that.

Three observations of a more practical kind, which I hope may help us to pray, asking: first, about praying for little things; second, about praying for vast things; and third, about praying for local things.

By "little things" I mean the things that *will* come into our minds when we try to pray, though we never intended to think about them. We can do two things with them: suppress them, and conduct a frustrating and unhappy struggle; or accept them and make them the subject of our prayers. It's not a bad rule of thumb: when you find yourself thinking about it, pray about it. And if as you try to frame a prayer you find, as you feared, that it is altogether too base — after all, you don't need the money; you just can't stand your colleague being one point higher on the scale! — that is the first step to ordering your unruly will to something less ignoble. Desires are like seeds; once put in the soil of prayer under the sun of God's attention, they begin to sprout upwards. "Why can't I be as important as Joe?" grows into, "Lord, help me to see that what I am doing is valuable!"

By "vast things" I mean World Famine and Disease, Third World Debt, and other things with capital letters; noble, worthy things that we turn our minds to at important seasons like Christian Aid Week, which very suitably occurs at Rogationtide. Now, the temptation here is to indulge our penchant for such objects too readily. They are so grand, sweeping, and universal that they flatter our idea of ourselves as those who carry the needs of the whole world on our hearts and participate in the magnificence of divine providence. Furthermore, because they fall (to our conception) into the category of "things that cannot be changed", we pray for them without a serious engagement with the *practical* character of prayer. There are those who would bristle with intellectual disgust if you urged them to pray for rain in Oxfordshire, who will with the greatest complacency pray for relief of drought in Africa! What is needed here is to bring some concreteness to these large ideas.

A few weeks ago Canon Peirce took the opportunity of a sermon at the Eucharist to describe to us in exquisite detail a Sunday lunch enjoyed as a guest in an Archdeacon's home in Zaïre. As he spoke, all the capital letters fell away, and we saw through his eyes a serious, devoted family with tasks, satisfactions, and anxieties different in circumstance but very like our own in *timbre*. When he prays for that church, it will not be very different from praying for the family in some vicarage in Oxfordshire. Each of us needs such links as these to make our prayers concrete, to help us take responsibility in detail for the generalities we find so elevating in the universal.

The little things have, as it were, to be let grow bigger; the vast things have to be brought down to earth. They must both be more like "local things", that is to say, like institutions, people, projects which form the context of our lives and among which we commonly assume our responsibilities: our church, our University, our business, our neighbourhood, our home and family. But precisely because we do assume responsibilities in these contexts, they can become the most difficult to ask for. They can all too quickly be things "we can change" — so that it seems altogether mean-spirited to pass them on to God. Or they can be things "we cannot change", to which we must simply resign ourselves. We are, in fact, rather possessive of our own fields of action, quick to find some high-minded way of warning God off. Precisely for that reason we never *envisage* our field of action properly. It doesn't become a question to us; we don't bring our imagination to bear on it. Imagination is a divine gift if ever there was one; it is being lifted out of our own perspective, given a new pair of eyes. So that even if it were true that all these "local things" lay within our own powers, and needed in principle no other powers than our own — and that, of course, is far from the truth — those powers would still be unfruitful and unproductive until God fructified them with the gift of insight and imagination, which we need to ask for if it is to be given.

There is one striking example of this on our doorstep at the moment — the financial crisis of the Church of England. You will have heard it discussed from every conceivable point of view: as a thing we can't change, as a matter for anger at managerial incompetence; as a thing we can change, an opportunity for us all to pull together, sharing the burden. But I have not heard it put about as something to *ask for,* an invitation to persistent and obedient prayer. We have prayed this week for a just distribution of the world's resources, so that others may have what they need. We have not begun to pray that our church may have what it needs. It is too close to us, too much a presumption of our lives, too much, if one may put it like this, a real *necessity* for us to see it as a likely *project.* But unless we do pray, we shall not learn to imagine it rightly as a need. You will soon hear from the Dean and Chapter about a very modest scheme we contemplate to enable the Cathedral to play a small part in the Diocese's response to the financial challenge. We shall be asking your help, and I must confess that I conceived this sermon as an opportunity to — how shall I say it? — soften you up? prepare the way? But you see at once that I cannot possibly do that! The message of Rogation Sunday stops me in my tracks. How could I rush into talk of us all doing our bit and sharing the burden when my task, and yours, is so clearly set before us? We cannot escape it; we cannot improve on it; we have simply to learn to ask God. *Ask, and it will be given you.*

Coming to Mount Zion

You have come to Mount Zion and to the city of
the living God, the heavenly Jerusalem, and to the
innumerable angels in festal gathering, and to the
assembly of the first-born who are enrolled in heaven,
and to a judge who is God of all, and to the spirits
of just men made perfect.   HEBREWS 11:22F.

The church calendar has given us quite a week. On Thursday it was All
Saints Day, closely followed, as the Middle Ages bequeathed it to us, by
All Souls, the commemoration of faithful departed — a sequence that
suggests too easily, it must be confessed, a distinction between high-
flying and run-of-the-mill Christians. To this medieval diptych the
Protestant churches prefixed on All Hallows Eve a commemoration of the
Reformation, a suitable antidote to the notorious superstitions of that
day, and this has of recent years found admission to the Church of England calendar. A less recent arrival there, but not by much, is the commemoration next Thursday of the Saints, Doctors, and Martyrs of the
Church of England, and if that were not enough, yesterday was assigned
to the most eminent of Anglican doctors, Richard Hooker. This constella-
tion of memorials has led me to think about *the spirits of just men made per-*
fect, a theme given a certain poignancy by a service at St. Margaret's,
Westminster, on Wednesday to give thanks for the life of Stephen Neill,

4th November 1984.

The Community of God's Word

one time Bishop of Tinevelly in India and one of the great unofficial statesmen of the twentieth-century church, who until his death in August at the age of 83 would regularly be found in our midst here on Sunday evenings at Evensong.

We believe in the *perfection* of the saints, that it is God's purpose to cleanse his church from every spot and wrinkle and make it, finally, a worthy partner for his Son. We believe that this destiny is for all, that there is nothing tolerated in the heavenly Jerusalem to spoil the wedding of the Lamb. It is an aspect of Christian hope which seems clear enough from a distance, less so from close up, like a mountain range that rises sharp and distinct from the plain when viewed from twenty miles away, only to dissolve, as you approach it, into foothills. Let me illustrate by asking four questions about this perfection:

Is it moral perfection we are talking about? Apparently so, because only a moral perfection will redeem the human being and so fulfil God's purpose for restoring mankind in Christ. Yet when we look at the saints we often see achievements accompanied, even assisted, by moral failure. Think of the great figures of the Reformation: was it not their intemperance and impatience that gave the driving force to what they accomplished? If Luther had had that loveable virtue we describe as "being a good listener", would anything worthwhile have happened in Germany? If Athanasius had been a "fair-minded man", could the dangers present to the church in Arianism have been warded off? There is in the saints a tension between a perfection of being and a perfection of doing.

Is it a uniform perfection we are talking about? Apparently not, since the perfection of the saints must reflect their individualities, enhance their unique personalities and special gifts. We find it insipid to portray great figures of the past "like plaster saints", ironing them out into a preconceived pattern of virtue. Yet perfection is not simply the enhancement of personal idiosyncrasy. The perfection of Oliver Cromwell does not mean warts grown to infinite size. It means that in some way the warts fit the composition of the face, making a whole of beauty. God deliver us from a heaven in which Cranmer is more irresolute, Laud more tyrannical, Cowper more melancholic! Perfection means overcoming weakness by strength, even though the weakness is encompassed, not simply cancelled out. Beauty is not a feature of any and every object that exists. To be beautiful is to conform to a measure, which requires the correction of what is ugly.

Is perfection progressive? It may appear so, since our path to it involves growth and learning. We are to *grow in the grace and knowledge of our Lord and Saviour* (2 Pet. 3:18). Yet in how many saints do we have to acknowledge deterioration? Those who enter old age are especially exposed, because the temperamental and physiological changes that accompany aging do not make everybody nicer. The very traits of character that once made someone great can become a liability. Fierce determination with reduced flexibility of mind can become a weakness where it was once a strength. This, the central grief of old age, is well known to us. But it is not just a matter of upward curves or downward curves. The biographies of saints take on extraordinary shapes, and of this Stephen Neill was a good example. A long career of remarkable achievement, displaying exceptional gifts of intellect and hard work and also great personal warmth, especially in kindness to the young, was broken down the middle by a moment of spectacular failure in 1945, when he had to resign his bishopric and return from India to Britain. On either side of that humiliation were two fine careers: that of the gifted, self-assured young missionary, for whose energies the glories of an English University provided too little scope, who therefore betook himself to India seeking to devote great powers to great tasks; and that of the elder statesman ex-bishop, a founding father of the World Council of Churches, ceaseless author, relentless globetrotter, counsellor, evangelist, and scholar, making the world his parish in a way John Wesley could not have dreamed of. Manifestly the same man, with the same virtues and the same gifts, yet what gave shape to the whole and turned these gifts into global channels was a single hammer-blow of failure. How can such a career be accommodated in our idea of progress?

Is perfection complete in this life? It might appear that it was not, so obviously do the finest of those we lay to rest show traces of weakness to the end. Medieval speculation conceived of a further period of perfecting after death, the "purgatory" so memorably celebrated by Dante and so infamously exploited by the indulgence-merchants of Luther's time. We can see why such speculations developed; they were a serious attempt to address the paradoxes of perfection, and as such they were perfectly legitimate. However, they turned in the wrong direction. Instead of exploring the idea of perfection more deeply and unfolding its complexities, they took the idea for granted and projected a posthumous state of affairs to accommodate it. That is why these speculations tended not to take this life seriously enough. They avoided asking how the Holy Spirit actually does use the conditions of this life to produce perfection, and what kind of perfection he produces — here and now.

I have spent so long on the questions that I barely have time to suggest where answers may be looked for. First, to conclude our quotation: *You have come . . . to the spirits of just men made perfect, and to Jesus, the mediator of a new covenant.* At the heart of the Christian idea of perfection is this central point: we are perfected as we participate in the perfection of our representative, whom God raised from the dead, the *pioneer and perfecter of our faith* (Heb. 12:2).

There is, therefore, a perfection already implicit in the decision of faith, symbolised by our baptism. That decision, if allowed to shape our lives, will give them meaning and fulfilment, however ambiguous and shapeless they might otherwise appear. Think of the dying thief next to Jesus on the cross. What does that flickering faith in a dying man mean for the shape of his life? It means that it had a point — all of it, not only the last hours. The squalid years of violence and self-interest now led up to something, to that final meeting and moment of conviction. This formative decision gave shape to the ambiguities and contradictions that went before it. It overcame them by encompassing them for good.

Now, it is through that formative decision that individual gifts and achievements, the glories of the saints that catch our eye, acquire their meaning, too. Those giants are not autonomous, good in themselves. They are good as they are shaped by the decision of faith. St. Paul speaks of astonishing achievements on the part of himself and his fellow-apostles in these terms: *We have treasure in earthenware vessels, to show that the transcendent power belongs to God* (2 Cor. 4:7). The perfection of the great achiever is derived from what he carries with him: it is illuminated from within by the treasure of God's self-giving in Jesus. The achievements of the saints are celebrated as ways in which divine glory is seen in the world.

But what we say about the achievements of the saints we must also say about their sufferings and their limitations, their failures to achieve. Indeed, this is precisely what Paul has in mind with his earthenware-vessels metaphor. God who wrought the salvation of the world by the submission of his Son to weakness will show forth that gospel through the weakness of his saints; for once again their weakness gains its meaning from the decision of faith that shapes their lives. It is no longer just weakness; it is *carrying in the body the death of Jesus* (2 Cor. 4:10). Saint John reports words spoken by the risen Jesus to Peter: *When you were young, you girded yourself and walked where you would; but when you are old, you will stretch out your hands and another will gird you and carry you where you do not wish to go* (Jn. 21:18). It is a saying with many facets. It refers, says the evangelist, to Peter's martyr-death; but it also shows more widely a characteristic form that glorifying God takes in his saints, and especially in the old, which is trustful impotence. Within the context of Jesus' death even impotence and failure, meaningless and empty in themselves, can become ways for God's glory to pass. And even shame may have its place. The most mysterious thing said in the New Testament about the perfection of the saints is a throwaway remark of Paul's about those who have, by devoting themselves to misconceived undertakings, simply wasted the efforts of their lives. He speaks of such people as being "saved" like someone rescued out of a burning house, the flames of judgment exposing with ruthless clarity the worthlessness of their achievements. It is not a fate to be embraced; yet even through the torment of shame there is something that God can bring to perfection.

You have come to the spirits of just men made perfect, and to Jesus. As we follow that rule, we see why the perfection of the saints, like Jesus' own glory, is hidden from our gaze. *It does not yet appear,* says the First Epistle of John, *what we shall be, but we know that we shall be like him when he appears, for we shall see him as he is.* We must speak of a transformation still to be achieved, but we must speak of it not in terms of purgatory but as a transformation wrought by the clear, unclouded vision of the Son of Man. What we see here of the perfecting of the saints is a preparation for that vision, and the effect that vision has on us will reveal what we have become in the course of our lives. But to measure what we have become by the vision of the Son of Man is to test it for its humanity. The humanity that God gave us at first is restored and glorified in him. The question will be: what relation have we to that humanity? Have we clung to it in the exercise of our gifts and talents, in our

The Community of God's Word

achievements and our failure to achieve, or have we shrunk from it? That is the moral aspect of the perfection of the saints. The perfection of the saints is not their own individual perfection at all, but his — and that is the reason for our confidence as we lay to rest in his name those in whom we could still see many imperfections, and as we face the likelihood that our own lives will end before we have achieved or become what God has called us to achieve or become. To all these doubts and ambiguities we can pronounce a healthy, "Never mind!" *It is not,* said Paul, *that I have already attained or become perfect, but I press towards the goal . . . that I may be found in him, not having a righteousness of my own . . . but that which is through faith in Christ* (Phil. 3:12f.).

Frideswide's Place

"Follow me, and I will make you fishers of men".
And they left their father Zebedee in the boat
with the hired servants.   MARK 1:17F.

Space and place are both given us; we don't make either of them. But they are given us in different ways. Space just lies there before us, bounded only by its natural features. It waits for us to move into it, to do something to it, or perhaps just to pass through it. Here is a meeting of rivers and a natural ford, low-lying flood-meadows and a moderately elevated gravel promontory. We can build a monastery here, or set up a market. Or we can decide the climate is no good and take the boat downstream to Dorchester. Place, on the other hand, is a human gift, formed like sedimentary rock by the slow deposit of neighbourly experience through successive generations. Place consists of buildings, institutions, conventions, and authorities, of stories that recall what has happened and explain how things came to be as they are. When the scholars began to gather in the twelfth century, they were looking for a space; but they had to take on a place, with its own name, Oxenford, and with its own store of experiences and memories. Among them the memory of an act of Christian social witness four centuries earlier: a lady of high birth from the Midlands, who, to avoid a dynastic marriage, fled from her home and

20th October, 1991, celebrating the festival of Oxford's patron saint. Christ Church Cathedral was formerly the church of the priory of St. Frideswide.

started a religious community here. An act almost as featureless and uninteresting as the bustling market-town itself — yet it had caught the imagination of the burghers and rooted itself in local memory.

The scholars you can imagine yawning and giggling alternately as the canons of Frideswide's church embellished this provincial little episode for their instruction. Yet if they were ever to come to terms with Oxenford, they had to come to terms with Frideswide. Twice yearly they would solemnly present themselves at Frideswide's shrine. It was, as it were, the tribute exacted from them by the place where they had settled. And we continue to pay that tribute in what was Frideswide's house, long since taken away from her by the scholars. We remember her, not because of all the saints of the Christian past she is the most striking, but because she gave her witness *here*. To the conditions and experiences of this place we who live here must submit. The scholars were used to taking the broad view, surveying the universe as it were through the eyes of God. Here twice a year they had to survey it through the shortsighted eyes of their good neighbours. Making that effort they learned that you can still see God from the market-town, and you can still experience the sanctity of God's church there.

One thing the gospel teaches us is not to be imprisoned by our place. From Jesus' first proclamation of the Kingdom we are called to be up and off. *"Follow me, and I will make you fishers of men". And they left their father Zebedee in the boat with the hired servants.* A gospel love of neighbour is always on the move; like a hungry fire, Saint Augustine described it, consuming every next thing that stands in its way, carrying us from where we were to where we have not been. Frideswide, too, had to flee before she could settle, cutting herself loose from bonds of family loyalty which restricted her obedience to God. But that is only half the story. The other end of the parabola of mission is coming to rest. *That is why I left you in Crete,* Paul wrote to Titus (1:5), to build a community into a self-conscious reflection of the rule of Christ. To give that gift of ministry requires an act of identification. What the daughter of a Mercian prince did in the eighth century the scholars of the thirteenth had to do again. They had to belong to Oxenford to give us Oxford. When they failed, what they brought seemed less like a gift, more like an invasion. The line is often a fine one.

All of which could be repeated with the names changed in every parish. And every wise parish priest knows that a tribute is demanded by the place to which he comes; if he won't pay it, he will not succeed in making Christ known there. Still, there is another, opposite danger. Settling in can be all too delicious. Building links, penetrating skins of defensiveness, accumulating local lore, especially in a nice place with nice people, can dispel the consciousness of mission altogether. Making Christ known, with all the challenges the gospel brings to those who are content with themselves, can be forgotten in the luxury of "getting to know you, getting to know all about you". The scholars would have done Oxenford no good if they had not remembered what they came here to do. They had to win St. Frideswide over, not succumb to her. They had to make her the patron of the University, not the University the patron of her cult. To preach the calling of a holy Christian learning in a tongue that could enthuse the burghers of a Saxon market-town — yet to preach *that,* not some substitute that might be more marketable in middle England! Like Frideswide herself before them, they had to bring a *new* gift of the Holy Spirit, a *new* demand of the Lord of history. New, but familiar as the name of Christ is familiar. That is the challenge before all Christian mission. Provincially, the Saxon abbess met the challenge. High-handedly the Norman scholars met it. The question is, will we meet it?

*   *   *

Excellent things of old, O Lord, were spoken of your city, for your name and your temple sanctified its walls. So we who call on you from many places rejoice to be citizens of the Zion to come, whose temple is your very presence. Prepare us, we pray, in our many earthly homes for that home, where we shall bring you the tribute of our songs and thanksgiving.

The Community of God's Word

Tradition, Truth, and the Public

Horror

*I heard the sound of his words; and when I heard the
sound of his words, I fell on my face in a deep sleep.*   DANIEL 10:9

The angel's words made Daniel faint. Or rather, *the sound* of them made
him faint, because all he can hear at first is the sound, *like the noise of a
multitude.* It is not the roar of a natural force, you notice. Not the roar of
a storm or an earthquake or a flood or a volcanic eruption. It is a human
force, and yet as unintelligible and overwhelming as any natural disaster
could be. The confused roar of the millions of millions, of human life in
the mass, "the great swarm life of mankind" as Tolstoy called it, is as vio-
lating, as destructive of thought and action, as any of the elements, min-
erals, and metals by which the angel makes its visual appearance. All
anyone can do, confronted with that noise, confronted with the great
ethnographic shifts, the rise and fall of civilisations, is to faint. It arises
on a scale on which we do not know how to live. Perhaps when we read a
newspaper, we may sometimes experience a shadow of the collapse that
Daniel experienced then. Confronted by humanity in all its chaos, the
will and power to live goes out of us.

But the angel sets Daniel on his feet, and addresses words to him,
articulate words attuned to his comprehension, of battles, kings, dynas-
ties, and racial migrations, the shape of history as it looked to the Jewish
people on the underside. You and I may find this survey of ancient his-

---

29th September 2001, for the feast of St Michael & All Angels.

tory remote; it is not a period we studied in school, anyway! But the important thing for those who experience such events is simply that they are made *narratable*. The chaos becomes history. The human mind can now engage with it, and that, for Daniel and his despondent contemporaries, means they can learn how to live within it.

What is it that has made the difference? The disclosure of a purpose of God, a good end which providence will serve by that chaos of human disturbance. Historians are important to us; they instruct us how to find sense in the chaos and to live in it. They are, in a sense, moralists. The virtue of historical imagination (and it is an intellectual *virtue,* just as much as a capacity from telling truth from falsehood) is a form of the knowledge of the good. It grasps the good in events, the good that the actors hoped to achieve, and the good that God, the ruler of all actions, will bring out of them.

And that is why today we celebrate angels. Sometimes, not least in this passage, we brush up against the role of angels as warriors, restraining the blind forces of power, creating a space of freedom and openness. Yet it is not as warriors that we are called to think of them here, but as messengers — and that is the meaning of the Greek word, *angelos.* For historical imagination must be made possible. It is not a virtue that simply springs up naturally without help, for it has to grasp the purposes of God. *I have been sent to you.* Sent to bring knowledge of what *will make sense* of this swarm-life of mankind, sent to bring us insight from outside it, a word of lucidity in our moment of confusion, an answer to give us heart in the midst of our despondency and collapse.

Freedom

Owe no man anything, but to love one another.   ROMANS 13:8

I must have read those words a hundred times or more, but I think I have only just understood them. I always supposed they meant: Discharge your obligations except the one you can never fully discharge, which is love. I was in good company in my confusion, for the New English Bible says something very much the same. But try reading it this way, starting from the previous verse: Discharge your obligations to all — tax where it is due, toll where it is due, respect where it is due, honour where it is due — but do not acknowledge any obligation that is not at the same time the obligation of mutual love; for every other obligation, including all those that the Decalogue lists, is included in this one commanding obligation.

Let every obligation be relative, relative to this ultimate one. Why? Because Christ the awaited king has come, assuming every structure of law and authority under his own law and authority, the law and authority of love. He *has come.* That is the cry of Advent. When Jesus the son of Mary came to John the Baptist at the Jordan, when he healed the sick and preached the law of love, when he presented himself confidently to the city of Jerusalem, the Gospels would have us realise that the time of waiting was over, the time of fulfilment was present. Don't be perplexed at the choice of a Gospel reading for Advent that we would more readily

---

3rd December 1989, Advent Sunday, during the collapse of the Socialist regime in East Germany.

associate with Passiontide; for the Passion is simply one angle from which Jesus' entry into Jerusalem can be seen. The other is from the prophet's cry at its centre: *Behold, your king comes unto you!*

And what happened when he came? He gathered, and has gathered since, a people around him; and that new social structure has put a question mark against all other structures of society that lay claim on people. It has not swept them aside, but has subordinated them. From then on there has been no true obligation that was not in some way the obligation that Christ has laid upon us: politics, family, university, art, the obligations of power and the obligations of powerlessness, all have become subject to that one obligation.

And what does that mean for those who gathered then, and have gathered since, around the King? Freedom! Freedom *from* the absoluteness and finality of those other obligations which we could not escape. Freedom *for* love, which allows us to assume those obligations again but in a quite different spirit of liberty. Freedom *in* conversion, in turning from the false lords to the true Lord, from the false absolutes to the one Absolute. On Friday evening the news bulletin contained the item that the East German Parliament had asked forgiveness of the Czech and Slovak peoples for their part in the Warsaw Pact invasion of 1968. That was the most unambiguous sign so far that there is real freedom in play in these turbulent Eastern European developments.

This Advent (who can doubt it?) belongs to Eastern Europe. It is given to *them* to turn *our* minds back to the gift of freedom. It is, of course, not surprising that there are ambiguities about what they have to tell us, both on their side and on ours. We learned, for instance, that after a week or so of free passage between East and West Germany the authorities had to impose strict customs checks, since so many East Germans were packing all their family antiques into a van and taking them to sell at mark-up prices in the West. That immediately raised a question as to how they conceived the freedom they had claimed.

But the question put to them is no greater than the question put to us, who are supposed to be in possession of this gift, the "free world". We can be forgiven, I think, a qualm at the sight of Eastern Europe apparently rushing into our arms. How have we understood freedom? How have we claimed it? What do we have to teach Eastern Europe about it with a clear and untrammelled conscience? The harder questions of Advent are put to us because they are directed at our pretensions, whereas Eastern Europe is in the happy state of abandoning pretensions and having nothing to defend. Perhaps the question put this Advent to us and to our Western friends is the even more shocking one: Which is the free world? Those who have long presumed upon their freedom, or those who are just discovering it?

If these questions caused us no qualms, we would be very thoughtless. But just at the moment I don't think we need mope over them. For if Christians who celebrate Advent know one thing clearly, they know this: whatever the ambiguities of this or that exercise of freedom in Germany, Czechoslovakia, Britain, or America, there is a true foundation laid for our freedom, and it cannot be taken away. The king who came to claim his own two thousand years ago while Tiberius reigned — and none too liberally! — has been given to us as the Lord who frees us from all other lordships, the debt which absolves all other debts, the law which validates and invalidates all other laws. To claim freedom for ourselves and for others today is to turn to that source of freedom and to raise the cry, *Behold, your king comes!* Give over your obligations to that one obligation, your loyalties to that one loyalty! Owe no man anything, but to love one another!

Cain's City

Cain built a city.   GENESIS 4:17

The story of Cain and Abel concerns the conflict between the herdsman and the agriculturalist. The author of the strange primeval history that forms the core of the early chapters of Genesis has, by placing the story in a certain context, exploited its haunting mythical resonances and brought them to bear on a perennial and universal question, which exercised antiquity as much as it exercises us today, that of the relentless march of civilisation. The initial idea was simple: Cain the agriculturalist, sheltered by God from the vengeance that would fall upon his head for his treatment of the herdsman, founds the first city. From him there springs all that we know of civilisation, music, weapons-technology, even a new line of herdsmen, no longer (the context suggests) innocent pastoral herdsmen such as Abel was but creatures and dependents of the civilised world. And over this flowering of the arts of civilisation there broods the harsh boast of Lamech, who glories in his ever-increasing power to defend himself against the environment that surrounds him. The myth of the farmer has become the myth of the city-dweller, with his civilised arts of culture and war, maintaining within his walls the elevated comfort of an artistic life and presenting to the outside world a bristling capacity for violence. There, says the great myth-teller, is the true meaning of the mark of Cain, the protection that God

---

3rd February 1991, during "Operation Desert Storm" to liberate Kuwait.

Tradition, Truth, and the Public

gave to the murderer to shield him from his fratricidal guilt. And this, he says, is the true meaning of civilisation. It is a perpetual struggle to ward off the memory of a primeval crime against the innocent.

Myths are powerful, and when we least expect them they come back to haunt us. Never has this myth come alive more vividly than in the last weeks. Tune in your car radio and make your choice between Jubal, celebrating the bicentenary of Mozart on Radio 3, and Tubal-Cain on Radio 4, explaining how his latest hi-tech weapons work. Cassettes and Exocets, they are the stuff of our civilisation. Everything about the present conflict evokes this myth with astonishing power; the terrain over which our engagements are fought is not far from where Cain slew Abel. The means by which we hope to achieve a victory are not very different from those of which Lamech boasted. But above all the myth dominates the perception of the conflict in a great part of the world, especially among those who oppose us. Large numbers of people who would be terrified and appalled at our enemy if they had to deal with him close up regard him as a kind of champion, since through him the ancient cry of Abel's spilt blood lifts itself to heaven once again to denounce the technological, civilised Cain who has destroyed a world of innocence and exploited the simple to reinforce his comfortable security. By mysterious spiritual suction we are all drawn in to play our part in the revival of an ancient drama. If our enemies prevail in this conflict, it will not be because of a greater might, but because of a greater myth, one with power to drain our conviction away from us and leave us guilt-stricken and irresolute.

Myths illuminate us, and it would be a terrible mistake to underestimate the illuminating power of this one. Much of what it suggests about the predatory and defensive character of advanced civilisation has truth — all too much truth! But myths also imprison us; they entrap us in a picture of ourselves where, it seems, any honest attempt to act in conscience, to respond to the needs and demands of our situation, will be hijacked as soon as it ventures forth. To be myth-bound is to be paralysed, incapable of action, reduced to striking the postures demanded of us. And the point of retelling a myth like this is not only to cast light on what we are and have been, but to liberate us from it. Certainly, this author's aim was to point us towards freedom, to a fourth son of Lamech, named Noah, of whom his father will say, *This boy will bring us relief!*

(5:20). And there is another, even more potent signpost: *At this time people began to call upon the name of* THE LORD. THE LORD! That is the covenant name, YHWH, by which God makes himself a partner with Cain's guilt-stained descendents. People called upon the name of THE LORD in prayer, through which the covenant partner gave them back their lost power to act and to do good, by acting with them. Here is a new element in the situation!

The most thought-provoking remark of this week, in my view, was about prayer. It was made on television by a Canon of Westminster who leads daily prayer-services for the Gulf War. He said, "I do not pray for the war as though it were good or right. I don't pray for victory". Whatever else he may have said was denied us by the news editors, so I don't pretend to give a reliable exposition of what he meant by his words, only of my thoughts about what I heard. And these were, first of all, to wonder what one *should* pray for — in public, on the assumption that there is bound to be some variety of perspective in the congregation, but then also, in private. For those most immediately affected, of course, *that* isn't difficult to agree to. But we can't stop there, because it looks like shoving the problem onto them, as though it were only *their* problem, not *ours,* as though I were not engaged in any way in a war that has imperilled or destroyed their lives, but merely a benevolent observer! If I am actually to pray for the Gulf War, I have to know what I think I am doing about it — supporting it or opposing it — and to what end, in either case. In the New Testament "praying" is synonymous with "asking", and "asking" implies making a personal commitment in deciding what it is you want to do, or to have done, or to happen.

St. James wrote: *He who asks must ask in faith, with never a doubt in his mind; for a doubter is like a wave of the sea. . . . A man like this should not think he will receive anything from the Lord. He is always in two minds and unstable in all he does* (1:6-8). The clergyman with the difficult task of leading congregational prayer can, to an extent, be cagey about how he does it. But we can none of us be cagey before God. It does no good to reserve judgment in prayer. Prayer is the way offered us out of the myth-bound paralysis. If we refuse to take it, we tie ourselves in more securely. In prayer God invites us to act again. He says, *"Rise, take up your bed and walk!* Venture something new! Forget that you are of all humankind the least fit to venture on anything — it is true, but not important! Forget

Tradition, Truth, and the Public

that you don't know everything, that you can't foresee everything, and that often when you try to do good you end up doing evil — it's true of what *you* do, but not true of what *I* do *with* you! Decide what good you will that we should do together, and I will correct and make good the defects and the blunders in your decision beyond all that you ask and think! But if you will not decide and ask, I cannot act with you, only apart from you."

Let me tell you, then, what I shall pray for until I know how to pray better. I shall pray for the speedy victory of the coalition forces, because I can see no other way to do good in the present state of affairs in the region. Speedy, because I am in anguish for the plight of those young Iraqi conscripts in the front lines, who will bear the brunt of the misery if there is a long ground war. I shall pray for a humane strategy of war on both sides; and I shall pray for a new will on the part of the governments of the region to tackle the bitter underlying resentments that have bred this conflict, especially the situation of the Palestinians. No doubt these prayers are too limited and partially blind. But I shall pray that God will teach me more about how he wills to bring good out of this evil. But I cannot *not* pray now, for fear I might think better of it later, because that would be to put up my guard against God and to close myself off from thanksgiving and rejoicing when he accomplishes the good, whatever it may be, that he has planned.

A visit with the children to the Civil War exhibition at the Commandery in Worcester taught me that when Cromwell reported his victory to the Parliamentary leaders, he referred to it, all matter-of-fact, as a "mercy" which God had granted. It is easy to say that this not-wholly-loveable saint might have achieved more spiritual insight had he learned to see the mercy of God in other triumphs than those of his own arms; but I don't think we are in a position to scorn the modest lesson in Christian faith he can teach us: if we act confidently, trusting in God, we shall be grateful for whatever accomplishment is granted us. I contrast with Cromwell's un-nuanced piety the notorious service after the Falklands Campaign, planned as a national celebration and carried off on a note of muted and sombre ambiguity. Political observers of the time thought this a rather clever way of denying the Prime Minister the little affirmation of her policies that civil religion could have offered her. I don't for one moment imagine that the motives were so petty. But I fear it reflected a deep spiritual impotence to grasp in thankfulness the meaning of what God had done. The leaders of our Church, never having committed themselves to the struggle for limited justice which we undertook, found themselves at the end too distanced from the endeavour to be grateful for the outcome, which meant not only the cessation of hostilities and the liberation of the Falklands, but also, as it has turned out, a political benefit to Argentina, too. Nor did they offer mourning as an alternative to joy. There will always be much to weep for in war, not only our losses, but the losses of the enemy and of those caught up in the struggle by chance or accident. Tears are required of us constantly; but so is joy, when the immediate cause of tears is taken away, especially if the deeper underlying injustice that caused the immediate cause is taken away at the same time. Ambivalence is neither rejoicing nor mourning. It is an incapacity for either, a kind of ice age of the soul which cannot or will not commit itself to striving for a concrete good.

Churchmen, do not make the same mistake again! Criticize bluntly when political or military leaders do wrong; praise and support generously when they do right! Commit yourselves in prayer for the best outcome you can discern, and if God grants success to your endeavours, be genuinely thankful. Do not preach the message of constant and unvaried accusation which Abel preaches! There is a new gospel message entrusted to you, a message of the covenant name of God, who has kept faith with Cain's descendents that call upon him. *Abel,* says the author to the Hebrews, *being dead, still speaks* (11:4). But the blood of Jesus *speaks more loudly than the blood of Abel* (12:24).

Tradition, Truth, and the Public

Civility

I saw no temple in the city. REVELATION 21:22

Those of us who are used to praying for harvest on Rogation Sunday
may have looked for a touch of rural earthiness about our worship this
morning. But our attention has been directed to the city. That is not
without its good sense, though. If we must pray for the essentials of life,
we must pray also for *civility* — that is, the condition of living together
as neighbours in an ordered and lawful community. Civility, too, is an
essential of life, a point that can hardly escape us while our consciences
are daily exercised with the moral paradoxes of war. To fail of civility is
to plunge into war. And the simple fact that we find ourselves plunged
into war, hating what we are doing, hating the necessity of doing it, per-
sisting only because the one worse thing would be to turn our backs and
pretend not to notice while the foundations of civility were destroyed
elsewhere and for other people, *that* is a reminder that civility is something we may never take for granted, but must always pray for as a gift. *I
urge,* the apostle said, *that prayers be made for all men, for kings and all in
high positions, that we may lead a quiet and peaceable life.* When we forget
to make that prayer, we have forgotten the terms on which our fragile
human existence is given us.

But to pray for civility, we must hope for it; and to hope, we must
have a ground for hope. Is civility our destiny, or is it, as some more

---

9th May 1999, against the background of the Kosovo crisis.

tough-minded versions of evolutionary sociology would make out, an occasional epiphenomenon that may dawn for a moment only to vanish behind the dark clouds of cutthroat competition? The Bible, it is said, begins in a garden and ends in a city. The last book of the New Testament concludes with the hope of an eternally enduring civility. Not with another garden, because the goal of our redemption is not a return to innocence, but an acquired maturity, the work of a culture grown transparent and obedient to the purposes of God. Not with a family, where we would often like to find our ideal sociability, where tolerance, sometimes delightful and sometimes abrasive, is supported at all times by natural affinity and affection. A certain inauthentic haze of nostalgia blurs our vision when we try to spread family-emotion too far abroad. The "church family", the "European home", the "family of nations": they can all be ways of not facing up to the real conditions of civil existence, which have to do with respecting *neighbours.* Then, thirdly, it is worth reflecting, the Bible does not end with a church. Karl Barth observed: "The hope in which the Christian community has its eternal goal consists . . . not in an eternal church but in the *polis*". He had in mind, of course, the closing vision of John of Patmos's Revelation, part of which was read to us this morning: *I saw no temple in the city.*

John of Patmos is the great New Testament panegyrist of civility. There is no other witness in the early church who takes the subject with the burning seriousness that he does. Himself the victim of a failure of civility, a prisoner of conscience, he could very well have given up on civility, turning for consolation in some other direction, to the church, for example. Yet, remarkably among the New Testament writers, he is uninterested in the church. The word "church", in its "catholic" meaning as the universal community of Jesus Christ, simply does not occur within his book from the first page to the last; he speaks only of particular "churches", i.e. congregations, and that only in his introductory letters. What John is interested in, on the one hand, is the utterly authentic and truthful individual, the one who will give his life for truth, *the conqueror,* as he calls him — and, on the other, is the condition of civility appropriate to a community of such individuals. All around him are political forms that cater to the craven, the mindless, the easily manipulated spirit of mass humanity, forms of civil organisation stained with the cruelty of the dull-eyed crowd roaring for the blood of the dissenter. To

Tradition, Truth, and the Public

John of Patmos we owe the first serious attempt in Western history to notice and describe the workings of the totalitarian state. And a striking description it is in the light of our twentieth-century experience, pointing with brilliant clarity to the role of ideology in the false civil consciousness, and to the confusion of political with economic goods.

But John of Patmos can be difficult to read, partly because he is the only New Testament writer with a truly poetic imagination. Which is to say, he thinks not in propositions and arguments, but in images, which he uses not as a rhetorician does, as bait for the visual imagination, to impose a certain view of things upon our minds, but as a poet does, to discuss with, so that they constantly shift and change under our eyes. Again like a poetic rather than a discursive thinker, he has an astonishing sense of literary form, unparalleled among the New Testament writers. The sequence of visions in his book — "the Revelation" he calls it, in the singular, for though it is a sequence, it is a crafted unity — is as carefully balanced as a Mozart symphony. I cannot, I am afraid, conceal a certain enthusiasm for John of Patmos, which some of you may think reprehensible and others impudent. Of course, it is impudent for a preacher to indulge his enthusiasms in the pulpit; and it is also impudent, as Kierkegaard taught us, to praise an apostle as though he were a genius — like celebrating St. Paul as the finest upholsterer of the ancient world! Yet sometimes an apostle may have a touch of genius about him, and sometimes it may help to point that out, if only to clear away certain difficulties.

And John presents difficulties. When I was a child of six, my mother judged me ready for *Alice,* and I was set down to read in a safe place one day while she went shopping, confident that with such entertainment I could do no mischief. Returning, she found me bored and bewildered. I had tried to make my way through that sentimental preface about childhood which Dodgson ill-advisedly wrote for his adult admirers. Something like that can happen with Revelation. A century ago it became a fashion to take an interest in the short letters to particular churches which John attached to the front of his book, letters dashed off in haste to apply the contents of the vision to their several situations, written in a slightly fretful tone. They are the worst introduction to him. My advice to the reader is to start at Chapter 4, with the vision of creation. Then look ahead to the great closing vision of the city, and then tackle the story of history which leads from one to the other.

John's visions are often discussions with other literature, which he counts on his readers to know. So, when we hear, *I saw no temple in the city,* our minds are meant to leap to another vision of an ideal Jerusalem, that of the last nine chapters of Ezekiel, where the city *is* a temple — there is nothing else! Then we shall know that when John says he saw no temple, he is correcting Ezekiel. The two agree on a central point, however. In a city worthy of the name the task of worship embraces all other tasks. What marks the civility where the truthful and courageous individual can be at home is not, as conventional wisdom in the West has had it since, shall we say, 1791, a "secular" detachment from matters of ultimate importance, a studied neutrality about things that make life meaningful, a self-limitation of the politics to the surfaces of life and an avoidance of the depths. It is precisely the opposite. It is the transparent sovereignty of God that makes true civility possible. John's book of visions began with the heavenly throne occupied indistinctly by a divine creator, and ends with that throne occupied distinctly by God and the Lamb, that is, the slain and risen Jesus. This has been the outcome of the self-disclosure of the Creator through the contradictions of history: the human community as the place where God dwells, where the Lord is at one with his people. As the throne was surrounded by worship at the beginning, so it is at the end; but in place of the undeveloped energies of the created world symbolised by animal figures, the worship is offered by those who, articulately faithful in the struggle of historical existence, have earned the title of "his servants".

But John is eager to avoid one apparent implication of this: that the civic is swallowed up in the religious. I saw *no* temple. Here is the difference between a *Christian* idea of worship and that of a Jewish exile in Babylonia. Like the author to the Hebrews, John holds that the cultic worship of God has a *shadow* of good things to come, not the real form (Heb. 10:1). The presence of God means a withering away of such symbolic structures. It is sheer presence, the absolute being-there of God, to which nothing can be added. Worship itself, as he describes it, is not a religious performance but a matter of vision and identity, a worship that has emerged from behind the rood screen and become political. Therefore the temple disappears from view, like a shadow shrinking back at noonday into its source. It does not disappear into the city, as in Ezekiel the city disappeared into the temple. For the temple is not the city; it is

Tradition, Truth, and the Public

the Lord God the Almighty, and the Lamb, and the temple disappears from view because God himself is open to view. The city, on the contrary, does *not* disappear from view, for the city is not a shadow cast by the Lord God the Almighty and the Lamb. The city is his covenant partner, the human race *with* whom and *for* whom he has sworn eternally to *be there* in civility.

Ezekiel's city-temple is the source of a river that flows eastwards down to the Dead Sea Valley, where it restores all the blighted life which has never had a chance to flourish there since God's judgment on Sodom and Gomorrah. John's city has a river, too, but it does not flow *out of* the city, but *through* it. It proceeds from the throne of God and the Lamb, and flows through the city square. For John, civility is not the *source* of blessings to humankind; it *is* the blessing which humankind is given, and it springs directly from the rule of God, from the throne, which has been a constant presence throughout his visions, but is now for the first time called "the throne of God and the Lamb", for it is the achievement of God's redeeming work in Christ. And the channel of blessing, the river, is understood by John as the Holy Spirit. From God arises our common life, and in God.

By the light of this city the nations walk. And this we may find puzzling. What nations? How can there be an *outside* to this destiny of civility? Jerusalem, the city, *is* the human race restored in all its universality. Yet — and this illustrates John's argumentative, rather than static, use of images — it is also the *elect* people, Israel, chosen to be the *dynamic core* that restores the Gentile world-order. Israel's movement out into the world and back, shedding light on those who sit in darkness and in the shadow of death, is not simply left behind. This is a matter of importance to John, who has given a delicate turn to Ezekiel's detail about the leaves of the trees being for healing, adding *for the nations.* The city is indeed the destiny of all mankind, but not *self-contained* as such; it is the focus of a world of diverse activity, in which the natural glories of the kingdoms are brought in through its open gates and allowed, as nature's glories must be, to give the answer of human praise to the glory of God streaming out through them. How can there be kings and nations any more? Because every good structure of nature, even those altogether imperfect forms of national civility we have known, point back to one source. The natural energies are "outside" the city, because they are always coming in. The great civic stage has its ampitheatre. All human energies and creativities and powers are unified in the city, but not swallowed up or enclosed there.

Only one thing is missing from this eternal commerce of nature and civility. *There shall enter no unclean thing.* John has chosen his words carefully at this point. They do not mean that there is an alternative "somewhere", where evil may have independent existence apart from the city. There is no final compromise of good and evil, no ultimate coming to terms. No unclean thing shall enter the city because no unclean thing remains in the world to enter it. All that lies beyond its gates walks by its light.

How may we be nourished in a time of war by this vision of eternal civility? Let me make three brief suggestions.

First, we will learn that what we call "peace" is in fact "civility", a condition of civil life, not merely the absence of strife. It is the possibility of ordered and lawful living together. And as such, tolerance is not a sufficient condition for it. There is a necessary place for tolerance in peace, but a necessary place for intolerance, too, a point at which the words, *no unclean thing shall enter it,* define the integrity necessary to its existence.

Secondly, this peace and civility is not simply available to us, at our disposal. We cannot plan for it in the way we can plan for economic growth; we cannot campaign for it as we may campaign for Scottish independence; we cannot legislate it as we may legislate for the outlawing of foxhunting. The worst folly in a time of war is to insist that war is all a stupid mistake. Those whose imaginations cannot rise to the issues, who must therefore reduce the issues to the scale of their imaginations, are always quick to announce that a very little bit of common sense would have avoided the situation altogether, a very little bit of good will would quickly find a way out. This combination of wishfulness, boastfulness, and general irritability with everyone who bears responsibility is actually sheer unbelief. There is an important place in war for confessing our sins, both great and small. There is no place for suggesting that peace is, after all, merely commonsense. It is nothing if not the self-bestowal of God upon mankind, to make mankind one civil community. For that we can only wait, hope, and pray to be worthy of it.

Thirdly, however, we can and must prepare ourselves, in spirit and in

Tradition, Truth, and the Public

act, for a life of civility. We can and must pursue the virtues that it demands of us, the habits of mind without which it can never be entered. These are an unbending commitment to speaking the truth in public, a willingness to accept isolation and public rejection, if that should be its price, and, above all, the worship of God as the source of common life, "political worship" as the Germans like to call it. Our civic destiny may transcend all forms of worship and religious practice, but the worshipping awareness of God and of the self before God is indispensable to it.

The mind-set of the flesh is emnity, says Saint Paul. A political and social culture that makes a virtue of confining itself to the flesh and avoiding the spirit, is, in the end, nothing but systematic preparation for war. And that is how our enemies at the present time and in other recent engagements see our posture. That is the reason they cannot credit our officious good intentions in attempting to preserve them from self-destruction. Can we be surprised at this? Does it not actually tell us of a deep spiritual tragedy of the Western world, a tragedy perhaps deeper than anything now playing out in grief-stricken Yugoslavia: that we have gazed upon the eternal city, have learned to love its aspirations, but have then turned away in impatience from its spiritual disciplines?

Knowing the Truth

My teaching is not mine, but his who sent me;
if any man's will is to do his will, he shall know
whether the teaching is from God.   JOHN 7:16

After ten days in which nobody has talked about anything except the international situation I almost feel I need to apologise for asking you to think about knowing and teaching the *truth*. Who can afford the luxury, we may think, of frivolous doctrinal quarrels, when all our efforts must be bent to discerning what the situation requires should be *done*. Yet the subject seems less remote when we reflect on what the situation really is. The conflict between the Western world and the Islamist radicals is nothing if not a doctrinal division, a disagreement about the truth of the world and the truth of civilisation. If ever there were a war of the world-views, this must be it; and we will not engage in such a struggle for long before we have to face the question of what convictions we are struggling for, and how we can be sure of them.

At a time of crisis, moreover, it is right that we examine the ways in which we ordinarily spend our days. And a University spends its days upon discernments of truth. Crouched over our word-processors, tapping out sentences on the keyboard, looking back at them, correcting a word here and adjusting a phrase there, forward-spacing, backward-spacing, copying and pasting, over and over again, hour after hour, all in

---

23rd September 2001, following the terrorist attacks on New York and Washington.

order to get it "right". And by "right" we mean "true" — as true as it can be made, as free of misleading suggestions or possible misunderstandings, as balanced in its presentation of reality, as sharp and focussed in its expression. At risk of curvature of the spine, malfunction of the bowel, loss of sight, and a thousand other physical ills, we labour to tell the truth; or we pore over books and documents, scan the lines, check the references, mark things for approval or correction, note down what must be retained and remembered, all in order to know the truth. It cannot be so very secondary a matter, to us at any rate, this knowing and telling of the truth, if it forms our chief business and shapes the institutions in which we work. But neither is it so secondary to others. The desire to study and learn, to clarify and express, consumes the unlearned as well as the learned. Most of us will have met someone, wholly engaged, and perhaps successful, in active pursuits, who is driven by a passionate longing to get back to the study of the truth. It is a human goal, something which we all need to do in order to live well.

Yet there hangs over the subject a cloud of doubt and suspicion, whether our labour for the truth is spent in vain, whether the truth can, after all, be known, whether the very idea of truth is too elusive philosophically to afford us a goal in life. Our discomfort with these thoughts makes us play down the issue of truth. We prefer to conceal our interest in it, to treat it lightly, assuming an air of modesty and unpretentiousness which is, in fact, a cloak for insecurity. We are distressed, but can hardly be surprised, when society's paymasters notice our evasions and undervalue our efforts, which we ourselves do not know how to value properly. Strong doctrinal truth-claims, on the other hand, such as underlie the project of our civilisation's enemies whoever they may be, may have a special importance for us precisely because they do not allow themselves to be concealed and hidden away. They force themselves on us rudely, and, as they do so, force on us the unwelcome question of ourselves and our truth, which is to say, what we think we are about.

The claim of Jesus, as St. John presents it to us, is uniquely uncompromising: not only to teach the truth, but to be the truth, the Word of God revealed in human life. This makes him the paradigm teacher of the truth, speaking the truth that he is. He is the centre around which the universe of truths, God's own universe, revolves. His teaching is the model of all true teaching, and our acceptance of his teaching is the model for all discernment of truth. *He speaks as one who has authority, not as the scribes.* And he says, *My teaching is not mine.*

"Not mine" is the first relation that anyone ever has with the truth. In the moment of excitement when we first grasp a truth, we know the difference between discovering something and inventing it. There it was, waiting for us, but we have only just come level with it. It did not begin with us, but came to us. It is a gift given us by reality itself. And as we have not achieved it, so we are not in control of it. The truer our discovery is, the more we have still to learn about it. Discovering the truth is like being shown a door that lets us in on a world.

And as we experience this "not mine" in the moment of discovery, so we experience it also in the painfulness of searching. The search for truth is not merely a matter of finding words for what we really know. Certainly, the experience of fumbling for words, an experience which I find gets commoner as I go on, is one way that we become aware that the truth lies outside our control. But it is not only the expression that is beyond us; it is the truth itself, which must be given, and cannot be produced.

For truth is a relation between ourselves and what is not ourselves, and that relation cannot arise within the circle of our own critical exertions. Those exertions are real enough, to be sure. We observe carefully; we filter out errors from our perceptions; we pursue the question of our object single-mindedly and logically. Yet what we know is true is validated from outside us, beyond the circle of self-purgation. And we know too well that those same critical efforts that prepare us for the truth may also stand in the way of it. The objects we attend to are situated in a universe of events and relations, and these disappear from view the more closely we focus attention on our object. It is well-known counsel (isn't it?), never ask the expert the wrong question! The very fact of concentrating intensely upon *this,* means losing sight of everything *else,* and together with everything else "this" disappears, too, for it only exists, whatever it may be, in its proper place in the universe of truths. That is why truth is elusive. Our search for it has two poles, a mathematical point on the one hand, the universe on the other. The truth of the object we enquire about lies within the dynamic field between these poles, yet both are infinitely beyond reach.

In their efforts to belittle Jesus' authority the Pharisees posed the alternative: Is he properly taught, or only self-taught? *How is it that this man has learning, when he has never studied?* But Jesus stated the alternative differently: am I self-taught, or taught by God? In the end, this is the *only* alternative. If one does not receive one's knowledge as a gift, one constructs it as a private invention. What we have learned from others, how we have been trained, how we depend on tradition, massively formative as they all may be, can only be a preparation. Tradition is the path which leads to one or other of the two possibilities: we receive our truth as given, or we pretend to make it up. And we experience tradition in this way. It is inescapable, and it is precious; we speak proudly of our teachers and refer to them with gratitude; yet we know that everything they have done for us is only a preparation for the moment when we are on our own. We cannot be satisfied with repeating their teaching, and they could not be satisfied with it either. We must know something for ourselves, something that is "not theirs"; but that something must be "not mine", either.

To return to Jesus: how can it be that he, too, claims no ownership in his truth? How can the one who speaks the truth *that he is* receive that truth as a gift? Why is the incarnate Word of God not the exception to the rule, *my teaching is not mine?* Because the Word of God is, in his very being, sent forth. *My teaching is not mine, but his who sent me.* He comes from the source of truth, an emissary of the Father into the world. His being, like his truth, is not just a possession, but a mission. He is the truth and he is emissary of the truth. It is as unthinkable that he could be the truth of God and not sent as its emissary, as that the Father could own his truth and not send forth his messenger. The truth of God is a self-communicating truth. The Word of God knows no other truth about himself than that he is sent, no other knowledge of his Father than that he sent him. The Father's mission of the Son is the whole truth about God.

And we, too, receive truth not only as a gift but as a task. The task is as inexhaustible as the gift is. Every true thing we are given to say is only a prepayment on the truth that remains to be said. Each payment on our debt leaves the capital outstanding. For this is God's mission, which began before us and will continue after us. For the brief space of life we are privileged to be caught up in it. If we do not understand our relation to the truth in this way, there is only one other way in which we can think of it. *He who speaks on his own authority, seeks his own glory.* Instead of mission there is self-positing, thrustfully imposing ourselves, our conceptions, our ideas, upon the credit of others.

A great deal of would-be communication of truth is of this kind. It moves within the closed circle of mutual credit which St. John calls *the world*. We build up epistemic credit by satisfying other people's expectations, and so impose our ideas on them; we entrust our judgment to the epistemic credit of others, and put ourselves at the mercy of their ideas. The word *doxa*, translated "glory", means also "opinion"; and nobody in a University can fail to know how these two ideas are tied together and how strong a pull they jointly exert. Conventional expectations and recognitions permeate the whole fabric of the search for truth as we know it. A community of academic recognition quickly becomes a black hole in the universe, every ray of light bent back into an atmosphere too heavy to let it out.

Doesn't that metaphor illustrate my point? I picked it up, as is quite obvious, from overhearing conversations that went above my head. And many other things that I can tell you I have simply picked up, though more comprehendingly, perhaps, and more discerningly. Of someone offering surprising information I ask, "And where did you get that?", judging its reliability by the credit of its source. How can we break out of this in-turned, incestuous exchange of recognition? How can we avoid being pulled back into the world's gravitational orbit, and launch our probe into the deep space of the universe of truth?

Take heed how you hear, said Jesus (Mark 4:24). We have spoken of teaching first; but everything we have learned makes it impossible to think of teaching in isolation. For if we have understood what it is to teach the truth, we will know that it is, quite simply, to learn properly. Teachers are learners *first* and learners *foremost*. The criteria for speaking the truth are, in the last analysis, the same criteria as for learning it. They have to do with an attitude of will towards another will disclosed in reality. *Anyone who wills to do God's will shall know whether the teaching is from God.*

This should surprise us, for we are used to thinking of knowledge as clearer and more secure the further removed it is from the influence of will. On the one hand, we suppose, the object of knowledge is simply "what is the case", impassive and inattentive; on the other hand, the knower must be disinterested, filtering out the impulses of his will and distrusting them as contaminations. The will's business we conceive as lying outside the act of knowledge, driving us to seek it but not in contact with the operation of understanding. But that is not how Jesus presents the task of knowledge, according to St. John. To know the truth is to discern a meaningful and purposeful order of things, shaped by the operation of a gracious and benevolent will. And to discern it requires a kind of sympathetic atunement of wills: the will which bestows goodness and being must be answered by the will which worships and adores. The will to do God's will is a devotion to truth more demanding than the purely external motivation to find things out, so often celebrated in academic circles. For that too easily works out as a determination to colonise truth, to control it, to ignore one part of it in strengthening our control over another part. True devotion to truth is patient waiting on the will disclosed in reality, which is also the will to disclose reality to us.

And how do we achieve this will to do God's will? By waiting first upon the paradigm truth, the truth which reveals that the will of him who orders all truth is good to us, the truth of Jesus Christ, the Word made flesh. All dealing with the truth, we may say, is by way of being a prayer: Grant us, Lord, truly to know him in whom is hidden the truth of whatever we have been given truly to state.

Telling the Truth

O take not the word of truth utterly out of my mouth;
for my hope is in thy judgments.

Plato once suggested — and the suggestion has proved contentious —
that falsehood in speech was not so grave an evil as falsehood in the
mind. To speak untruth without believing it was better than to believe it.
Our modern instincts tend to the opposite view, to think deliberate deception worse, because deliberate. And our modern view might, at first
glance, claim support from the poet of Psalm 119, who was concerned
with the place of truth not simply in the *mind* but in the *mouth*. But a
closer look may bring the poet rather closer to Plato, and put him in a
more challenging posture towards some of our modern assumptions.

For truthtelling, in the first place, is a spiritual task that is set us. It is
not a state of equilibrium or rest that can be taken for granted. We tend
to suppose that truth is what we speak when we don't make a conscious
effort to lie. Truthtelling comes naturally; it is deception that takes hard
work. But the poet fears that his hold on truthtelling is something he
may all too easily lose. He begs to retain it. And that is not surprising
when you think how as children we have to learn the discipline of
truthtelling in the first place. Children lie, not because they want to lie,
but because they have not yet concentrated their minds on the business
of discerning and articulating the truth. Faced with the thunder of a par-

---

15th September 2002, returning to the same theme a year later.

Tradition, Truth, and the Public

ent or an educator, the panic-stricken child reaches for whatever fragments of fact or fancy may possibly serve to surmount the crisis. The younger child, exposed in the telling of some especially egregious fib, pleads, "It was a joke!" "No, it wasn't", we have to explain. "A joke is meant to be *amusing*." And what children do easily, so adults do under pressure. It is easy to think of ourselves as generally truthful, when all we have achieved is avoidance of those deceptions that involve the most extravagant outlay and the most expensive maintenance. Truth imposes disciplines of enquiry and self-criticism, disciplines which can quickly grow slack. The poet prayed to achieve a hold on truthtelling that would resist the pressure, so he might stand his ground with truth before critics and kings. It was to be his life-task.

It would be natural in this place to illustrate this task by referring to the life of a scholar, and pointing out how sustained intellectual engagement with a subject may become the central thread in a person's life. Natural, perhaps, but a bit indulgent! It does scholars good to be reminded that truth is not the private interest of a guild of professionals. It is the living concern of human beings, and the scholar's passionate interest in truth in one very narrow field often fails to generalise itself across life as a whole. For illustration I prefer to think of a young man I knew some years back, who was trying to cope with the emotional and relational devastation wrought on his childhood by his parents' divorce. At the heart of his difficulty was a sense of contradiction between a deep admiration for his very accomplished father and disgust at the way his father had behaved to his mother. This young man knew he had a lifetime's task ahead of him, learning to tell the truth about his parents with clarity and charity — *his* contribution, perhaps, to their reconciliation in this life or the life to come.

In the second place, our truthtelling begins from truth already given us. We tend to think that we find out the truth first and tell it afterwards; we do the experiment and then inform the waiting world of our conclusions. But no scientist stumbles into an experiment while brewing up coffee. The experiment is designed with a particular question in view, a question which springs from an initial apprehension of how things are, or might be. The scientist is led forward by the truth, proving it and clarifying it by experiment. Truthtelling follows reality, but it follows it like a hunter following game. It has it in its sights and slowly draws near to it.

And so it was for the poet, who started with something given him: *my hope is in thy ordinances.* The law of God pointed him to the truth he must tell throughout his life, like a figured bass on a page of music manuscript paper, presenting the skilled musician with the task of realising the text in a wealth of sound.

In the third place, our truthtelling is a function of ourselves, not only of our object. We tend to suppose that the object determines it all. We speak about situations or events past or present, facts observed or known by report, about what we have done and what others have done, and the truth of our speech depends on its success in bringing to light the way they really are and were. The searchlight of truth streams out from the speaker to illumine whatever is out there. Only, perhaps, when we find ourselves having to tell some very unpleasant truth about ourselves, do we begin to be conscious that it is not just a matter of directing the beam, but of turning it back on ourselves, so that it is we who, in the very act of speaking, are shown up. Every act of truthtelling is also a handling of ourselves, a self-telling in relation to what is real and true. *Take not the word of truth utterly out of my mouth.* The "mouth" is nothing more or less than the speaker. The owner of the mouth is determined by the word that it utters. Utterance is a self-disposal, in which we confirm or forfeit our capacity for reality, and with it our capacity for true existence. The danger is not simply that we may speak falsehood. It is that we may *be* false, and lose ourselves entirely.

Truthtelling is not simply a habit of precision of speech. Precision may in general be a good habit, though it can also be an irritating one if constantly indulged in. But precision can also be a screen which avoids truth. The essence of truthtelling is to use speech in such a way as to *clarify and reveal* both subject and object in their relation to each other. By it the subject becomes defined in relation to the object, not only the object in relation to the subject. And that is why for all of us in some manner the search for truth must shape our lives.

In the fourth place *truthtelling is one telling of one truth.* We tend to think of each occasion on which the truth must be told as discontinuous with the next, so that there is no connexion between this truth and that. But the poet envisages truthtelling as a sustained and unbroken practice, undertaken "continually, for ever and ever". *Take not the word of truth ...* For there is for him, in fact, only one word of truth, the word which gives coherence and connexion to the many and various truths we may tell from time to time, the word in relation to which the whole of our life is to be disposed. And since that truth which yields all other truths is the truth of God, we are all, in some manner, to be called "theologians". *God is not,* Saint Paul agreed, *far from each one of us.*

And in telling a large and complex truth there is difficulty and a challenge far exceeding the difficulty, great as it may be, of telling a single isolated truth. The difficulty is to determine how the various elements of truth belong together, in what order of importance; to determine which are the key interpretative truths, the truths about truths, round which the others group themselves. Here we may appreciate, perhaps, the point of Plato's insouciance in the face of verbal untruth. In attempting to do justice to a difficult set of connexions, we constantly encounter the need for forgiveness for our speech. There are accidents that befall us in speaking truth, "wrong things to say" which do not succeed in conveying the deeper truth of what we have in hand. These misadventures of speech are not themselves the decisive thing.

On the other hand, there can be "wrong things to say" which are not simply false, but are, in effect, falser than falsehood. A lie can be constructed entirely out of truthful elements. Think, for example, of a harsh and relentless critique of a piece of work, which takes no account of the author's abilities, experience, relative achievement in relation to others, etc. etc. Every detail in the critique may be irrefutable, yet the totality be the falsest thing that could possibly be said. As an older vocabulary had it, there is such a thing as a "specious" truth, one that lay entirely on the surface of the statement — undeniable and irresistible, yet suspect for its very obviousness, failing to lead us down to the less perspicuous structure of the reality we are looking at. Specious truth is convincing in a way blatant falsehood can never be — and yet may be more horribly deceptive.

In the light of these four orientations let me reflect briefly on the curious act of remembrance which we performed last Wednesday. What was this solemn national affirmation saying, and was it true? A year ago there took place a deadly assault on downtown New York and Washington, in which large numbers of innocent persons were killed, an act unpardonable by any standard of human justice. That is the specious truth of what was said in the act of remembrance, an undeniable truth, surrounded, however, by a broad penumbra of interpretation which was no less part of what was meant by it.

When we single out a past event for special commemoration, we affirm that it is pre-eminently important to our present situation. When we single out a past event for *public* commemoration, we affirm that it is pre-eminently formative of our collective identity. When we single out for special public commemoration an event that occurred *elsewhere,* we affirm that our bonds with that place are pre-eminently formative of our political identity. When we single out for special public commemoration an act of *hostility* done against that place, we affirm that we are tied to that place by shared resentment of the injury it suffered. The commemoration of last Wednesday was thus an assertion of Western solidarity as a defensive alliance, an alliance shaped by common resentment of hostility and a common sense of being under attack. This was no mere subtext, left to be inferred. Mr. David Blunkett speaking for the government declared that to pay due respect to the victims of a year ago was to be prepared to defend democracy against all threats. Our political identity, we notice, is no longer found in historical communities, America, Britain, Germany, or whatever, but in an organisational ideal, "democracy". The media pundits called on to improve the occasion were not slow to inform us that the name of the enemy of democracy was "religion". For religion, as the BBC psychologist ingenuously explained, shaped our identities. Naturally, all historical identities are inimical to the clothing of the West in its new ideological identity, that democracy which the solemnities of September 11th bind and commit us to defend.

Every reflective person must wonder about this new self-definition of the Western peoples. But that question is now fearfully sharpened by the debate about a possible war against Iraq. The case that has persuaded certain leading figures in Western governments that a military assault upon Iraq is a necessity has not yet been explained in full to the public, so that you and I can earn nothing but ridicule if we assert loudly at this point that a good case does or does not exist. But we can know what a good case, were it to be made, would look like. It would not be about democracy, nor about the events of September 11th, 2001. It would be about Iraq, about its actions and demonstrable intentions, and about the many attempts to bring it to lawfulness that have patiently

Tradition, Truth, and the Public

been tried and failed. So we may form a preliminary judgment at least on the honesty of those who bring forward these painful memories from last year in order to urge on us a practical undertaking of the gravest moral seriousness, an undertaking unrelated to them in substance and in relation to any facts yet published precipitate.

The practice of public commemoration which our Christian forebears left us was, in its way, a spiritually disciplined one. Commemorations were built around mercies received from God, occasions of thanksgiving for deliverance. So the two world wars were remembered on the exact anniversary of the signing of the armistice in 1918, a day of deliverance from war. I can think of no precedent for solemn ceremonies to mark the very moment when an abomination was committed. For times of grave affliction, when there was nothing concrete to be thankful for, the older practice prescribed public fasting, which ensured that the first response to crisis would be critical self-examination. Our Christian forebears knew well enough that public acts fashioned identity. They also knew, I think, that identities founded on recrimination were always in want of an enemy, and that to be in want of an enemy was to be sure of finding one.

Last week we did that unprecedented thing. We seized on an abomination and made of it a symbol of our posture in the world. We committed ourselves to an alliance of power built on resentment of one isolated and — for all the horror of that moment — ineffective blow. Within hours of the end of the Johannesburg summit, which showed "democracy" incapable of shedding disproportionate wealth, comfort, and command of resources in the service of common necessity, that alliance solemnly presented itself to the world in the guise of an injured victim demanding vengeance. I find it hard to imagine where this illusory self-understanding will ever lead us, other than to deeds of great wickedness. *O take not the word of truth utterly out of our mouths!*

Glory

"Sir, we would see Jesus!"   JOHN 12:21

For Jesus himself it was a signal: *The hour has come,* he declared, *for the Son of Man to be glorified!*

"Glory" means to have the eyes of the world upon you. We speak sometimes of "publicity", though that is a tinny, unreverberant word for a tinny, unreverberant business. Glory is more than publicity. It is when the tasks you have to perform acquire immediate and pressing significance for other people. They wait on what you do; their hopes and fears are engaged with you; if you fail, they are cast down, while, if you succeed, they celebrate. You are their representative; you act for them, and they act through you. And then they constantly want to see you; they lie in wait to feast their eyes, or their television cameras, upon you as you pass by. And that erotic attraction is not the least curious aspect of a curious relation.

In every society there are those who are projected into glory; you can tell the character of the society by the kind of people it thrusts forward. With us it seems to happen most to football players. But it happens to politicians, too, and at a time of conflict like the present, to soldiers. That is important, because the strange capacity to "glorify" an individual and invest him or her with representative status is one of the things that makes it possible for a large number of people to live to-

---

6th April 2003, before local and regional elections.

gether under the disciplines and restraints of a law-governed society. We do not abide by law simply because it is written in our natures; we abide by law as the authority of the law is reflected back at us through representative persons. As our armies march once again across lands which our grandparents administered as colonial territories, we should remember what that phase of history taught us: colonial administrations, however well conducted, lack representative authority, and so create, and often fall victim to, deep social tensions.

Political systems have their moments of bonding, when the instinctual identification between a people and its representative is evoked. The coronation of a monarch used to be such a moment: the act of anointing invested the royal person with a special aura. Modern societies have a different ritual, the election, neither so mystical nor so morally elevating, but every bit as instinctual and subrational. Identification is sealed by excitement and collective feeling. The reflective observer gazing at this ritual must be disturbed by it, as one might be disturbed by a tribal war dance. Yet we cannot merely blame the politicians for it; it lies with the nature of society, and nature is sometimes repellent. But neither should we allow this undignified procedure to give us a sense of superiority over other times and manners, or imagine that this effervescence, because it is "democratic", gives us some moral entitlement to commit wanton crimes against humanity.

Let us learn about glory from the glory of Jesus. *The hour has come for the Son of Man to be glorified. . . . What shall I say? Father, glorify your name!* For Jesus there are two points of reference: his admirers and followers on the one hand, and on the other the Father, whose self-glorifying was involved in Jesus' glory. Not only was a people involved in what he had to do, but God, whose truth, the truth of creation, judgment and renewal, must be displayed through it. Two constituencies met in him: a scattered crowd seeking an identity, and a God with the sword of truth in his hand to divide between falsehood and truth, between justice and wickedness. In Jesus the identity of the crowd must become one with the judgment of God, moralised, purged of self-deception, fit for constructive service. One might say, without stretching words too far, that the glory Jesus looked for was that of a truly political responsibility. For it is the clear-sighted aspiration for justice that distinguishes the political representative from the representation of the football-ground.

Time and again, the Gospel writers tell us, Jesus shrank from publicity, from the glory his admirers tried to thrust him into. The point was to wait on the moment of God's self-glorification. He saw that moment coming, Saint John tells us, with the arrival of the Greek admirers. It signalled the dawning of the international purposes of God, a judgment not for his Israel alone, but also for the gathering nations.

But there was another reason for his shrinking. He understood that to represent others at the moment of God's judgment would mean suffering for them. To accept responsibility was to carry the weight of God's division between truth and falsehood in his own person. So Jesus' "lifting up", his "prominence", assumes its famous double meaning: it is glory, and it is humiliation, because the work that Jesus has to do before the eyes of all is to suffer. Many great deeds will spring from that suffering; but it is the seed of those deeds only because it is not itself a deed, but simply a suffering. Yet taken fully into his purpose of doing the Father's will, it *becomes* a deed, the most truly political deed, the founding of the new community upon the terms of God's own justice.

So what has the gospel of Jesus Christ to say to the political leaders who represent us, rule us, and take upon themselves all too eagerly the task of doing justice for us, as they rouge their cheeks and trim their eyebrows for the cameras? It is very brief. Simply: "There is your model! He who was lifted up, and will draw all men to him!"

Tradition, Truth, and the Public

Hallelujah!

For those of us used to the language of worship the word "Hallelujah" is commonplace. In Christ Church, to be sure, we don't find our sermons interrupted by spontaneous Hallelujahs from the pew. But they crop up pretty frequently in psalms and hymns and other music. We know the bouncy Hallelujahs of Purcell, the hand-clapping Hallelujahs of Handel, the etherial Hallelujahs of Stravinsky. So we may be surprised to learn that the New Testament is very sparing of them; in fact, the word occurs only in one place, in the nineteenth chapter of the Revelation of John read to us this morning. But there we meet it four times. Four crashing shouts signal the climax of history, God's victory over the corruptions of human culture. Four joyous songs of celebration take up where the lament for fallen Babylon has left off. Those who lamented the squalid dealings of empire were kings, merchants, and seafarers — interested parties, in fact. But now the prophet hears a "vast throng", the voice of universal humanity. The good of all has been vindicated over the interests of some. *Hallelujah!*

The first Hallelujah hails the effective justice of God: *true and righteous are his judgments.* The second points to its effects in history: *the smoke of the city goes up — for ever,* because it is the last word. And now that history's story is told, it is time for Creation to take up its praise. Angelic and animal beings, twenty-four elders and four living creatures, cry, *Amen! Allelujah!* Just that, and no more, for they have no story of their own to tell. They dwell outside the sphere of world history and its

---

26th January 2003. The invasion of Iraq began on March 18th.

events. But they confirm its victory, for the long shadow of sin, cast Mordor-like over all creation, has been turned back and lifted.

And so we come to the fourth Hallelujah, the climax of the climax. Again we hear the *vast throng.* But now its voice is reinforced with the roar of the ocean and the clapping of thunder. Earlier Christ's voice sounded like many waters, and the Father spoke from his throne like a thunderclap. It is the voice of God, Father and Son, that joins the whole human community in praise. And where John finds the Father and the Son, the Holy Spirit is never far away. Here he speaks in the opening summons, coming from the divine throne itself: *Praise our God!* From servants and God-fearers, *small and great* — not only God's servants, but also God-fearers! — God's Spirit evokes the truth of praise. For praise — yes, even the praise which we bring in the eucharist this morning — originates with God's Spirit and returns through him to God. Praise is truth given us and offered back to God.

What is the content of this climactic Hallelujah? It tells of the universal rule of God: *the Lord our God, the Almighty, reigns.* And of what does the rule of God consist? If we have journeyed with John through the Book of Revelation to this point, we will feel fairly well-equipped to answer that question. It is his conquest of cultural and economic oppression, his delivery of humankind from slavery and delusion, his vindication of people who are persecuted. Yes, but: Hallelujah! Now that all this is accomplished, God's rule has taken on a new aspect, one we could not see clearly in the struggles and torments of history. *Let us rejoice and give him the glory, for the marriage of the Lamb has come!*

This is a moment quite as unexpected and breathtaking as that earlier moment in Revelation where the victory of the Lion of Judah is announced, and we are shown *a Lamb with the marks of slaughter on him.* At that point victory leads to the paradox of the cross. Now it leads to the paradox of the wedding, the union of Heaven and Earth. For the great transition has been made. What appeared from the side of history as the defeat of evil and the division of mankind, is now seen to be the union of God and mankind. This mystery was secretly foretold in every culture through coronation rituals that set forth the crowning of a king as his marriage with his kingdom. But now it is brought to fulfilment in God's kingdom. All history has been a preparation for it, and the wedding can be announced, for the bride is ready at last, clothed in *the righteous deeds of the saints.*

There is much that we could say on this theme as the world trembles once again on the brink of war. But this one thing should be enough: war is terrible not simply because it is horribly destructive, though it is, but because it is corrupting. If there is war, our minds will be assailed by storms of passion: by fear, anger, hatred, distrust, grief, which have the power to make us — and others, too, but first of all ourselves — wicked. The meaning of this war will be the kind of human beings it makes of us, the kind of moral atmosphere we shall leave for our grandchildren to imbibe. And that will be determined by whether we keep before our eyes the destiny of human history, the Hallelujah of union, and by whether we are prepared to make our way towards that destiny by the only route, the Hallelujahs of judgment.

Judgment has the penultimate purpose of discerning and clarifying the right, rejecting the wrong; but the ultimate purpose of history is life in union, with God, with one another. Can this moment of division, we may wonder, the moment that is so looming and threatening now, accomplish the purposes of judgment? Can it discern and clarify right and reject wrong? That will depend entirely on how we conduct ourselves. I say, *We,* for though militarily it may be the army's war, politically it may be the leaders' war, spiritually it is your war and my war. We may not sit it out; we must engage in spiritual struggle, against injustice, tyranny, and lying, wherever and however they affront us. And where do injustice, tyranny, and lying reside? There is not only *one* place, which could be pointed out now before anything has happened. The Devil is not so lazy or unimaginative, and neither may we be. Our spiritual warfare will have to be renewed each day; each day we shall have to take stock of where the battle lines of truth and falsehood are drawn since yesterday.

Write this! says the angel to John, for the second time in the vision, signalling a word of blessing of special importance to us. The first time it introduced the well-loved words, *Blessed are the dead who die in the Lord henceforth!* If we find ourselves at war, there may be many dead, and we will have frequent cause to ask how we may claim that blessing for them. But here is a blessing addressed more widely, to "those who are invited to the marriage-supper of the Lamb!" Shall we have our eye on *that* goal of history? Then our courage before the forces of evil will not fail us, and we shall acquit ourselves with honour.

*   *   *

God, before whose secret counsel the prophet lamented and the angels proclaimed news of great joy, that in evil and in good alike your praises might be sung: Grant us in our day the gift of insight, that we may discern the purpose hidden in the changing of the times and the tumult of the nations, and follow with singleness of heart the hope you have given us in the healer of the heathen and Israel's glory, Jesus Christ our Lord.

Launched upon Life by God's Word

The Sea! The Sea!

The sea is his and he made it....

We can appreciate at once the negative side of this great statement: the sea is clearly not ours, and we did not make it.

We did not make it: the business of the mariner is an art and a skill, not a process of production. Certainly, it is "productive", in that it yields goods for the human community to enjoy. But the mariner's business is not manufacture — like, say, shipbuilding — in which dead materials are fed in at one end, the finished product comes out at the other. It is not cultivation, like agriculture, in which living potential is tended and cared for until it produces its fruit. The mariner does not transform his materials nor help them transform themselves. He leaves the tides and the waves as he finds them. He does not mould them, he does not tend them, but he navigates through and across them; they are his medium, not his resource. His great art is to cooperate with them. He relates to the ocean as we all relate, not to a given task or piece of work which we set out to accomplish, but to our lives as a whole. We cannot, whatever we say, "make something of our lives". Our lives are our lives, given to us, not made. We can only venture upon life's sea and brave its storms — that metaphor is a common one, and much truer. To be "launched" upon life, to encounter the greatest adventure given us, the adventure of

---

8th September 2002, on the occasion of a seafarers' conference.

being human, we need a certain kind of wisdom, and for that wisdom it is the mariner, not the craftsman or the farmer, who is our model.

Today, of course, the models offered to those who are entering upon life are usually those of manufacture: life itself is seen as a kind of mass-productive process for which we plan, equip ourselves, and carry through. And so it is not surprising, perhaps, that we are told that recruitment to the maritime life is at an all time low. For this is an age with little sympathy for the adventure of life, an age which understands making, as it understands buying and selling, but does not understand *becoming*. The art of the navigator is a kind of "becoming". What is gained by it is not an object, but oneself. By engaging with an element that is other than oneself, alien to oneself, indifferent to oneself, one wins a knowledge of oneself and a command over oneself that is essential to the freedom that living requires. The mariner does his share of planning and calculating; he reckons up the winds and the tides; but he knows better than to think that everything can be planned for. He knows what it means to live with an unstable and unpredictable element, and that is where true wisdom lies. While the rest of the world attempts to ensure that nothing unforeseen shall ever happen, the mariner attempts to ensure that he will be ready for the unforeseen.

We did not make the sea, and *neither is it ours.* It is an element that cannot be possessed, but only lived *with.* A splendid tradition in English law decrees that ground covered by the tide can belong to nobody. The mariner, of course, knows a great deal about owning and possessing. From time immemorial there has been a connexion between seafaring and commerce. The maritime ports have been the great communicative hubs of trade and circulators of wealth. To this day, when everything else seems to have changed, that has not changed: the sea remains the only effective means of transporting bulky goods over long distances. The fall in recruiting to the maritime life suggests not only that the life itself is not appreciated, but that its service to commercial prosperity is not appreciated either. Yet if it renders a service to commerce, it is not itself primarily a commercial life. The sea is not a commodity in which we may trade. It is the passage across which we may trade; though our possessions pass across it, the passage is not one of our possessions. There are various ways in which we can and should assign responsibility for the high seas. Countries may claim jurisdiction, coastguards may exer-

Launched upon Life by God's Word

cise policing functions, fishing fleets may parcel out grounds. We can and should be solicitous for much that goes on in the sea, to preserve fish-stocks or to prevent pollution. Yet the sea itself is bigger than our care and our solicitude; it refuses to be made, as it were, a ward of court. The herring shoals may vanish if we do not care for them; but in that vastly accommodating and inventive ecological universe something will move in to take their place, something, quite probably, much less convenient to us than herring, but not at all inconvenient to the sea. The sea is not ours that it should do our bidding and ensure our livelihood. It will follow the laws that God has laid down for it in detached indifference to our pleas and aspirations. And if we frustrate it at one point, it will return to punish us at another.

The sea is his, and he made it. The first implication of that great statement is negative. We learn the limits of our human prerogatives and powers in respect of the sea. The sea is our teacher — a hard and demanding one, too! — in the beginning of human wisdom which, as the proverb tells us, is *the fear of the Lord.* If we cannot learn this fear from that teacher, perhaps we are incapable of learning anything from anyone. But there is a positive side to the statement, too. It is not ours, we did not make it, but it *is his, and he made it.* What does it mean that the sea was made by God?

Let us not miss one point, so vast that we may possibly overlook it: the sea is an object of incomparable *beauty.* To do justice to the many facets of its beauty, the play of light and shade on its shifting surfaces, the mercurial range of its moods and behaviours, and, what always gets to me first, its amazing repertoire of musical sounds — would be a job for a poet, and I am not up to it. But beauty is a sign of God's handiwork. And the peculiar beauty of the sea lies in the delicately poised balance it maintains between sheer chaos and calm order. The sea, as the Bible understands, is the closest thing on earth to primordial chaos. Of itself the element has no form, no borders, no stability; it affords no point of rest, no place for the sole of the foot. Yet it is *bounded* chaos, for God has drawn the coastlines round it, giving it its sinuous shape, and has pinned it in a press between the upward thrust of the ocean floor and the downward thrust of the weight of air. He has made, as it were, a frame fit for the most unframeable of elements, so creating that fragile equilibrium of wilderness and containment that pierces us to the heart.

We find the sea beautiful because it points us back behind the realm in which we are in control. The coastline "frames" the sea, and yet the sea frames the land. At once surrounded and surrounding, the sea makes us feel the intrusiveness of human beings, those cheeky latecomers to the drama of God and creation. *Where were you,* we hear God saying to Job (38:9-11), *when I wrapped the sea in a blanket of cloud and swaddled it in dense fog, when I established its bounds, set its barred doors in place, and said "Thus far may you come but no farther; here your surging waves must halt"? He made it,* and not for us but for himself and his glory. His handiwork lies beyond us, beneath us, above us, altogether out of our reach. We depend upon it, not it on us. Many common proverbs and metaphors remind us that our dealings with the sea are a kind of overreaching, a stepping where we have no point of purchase. We speak of being "at sea" over something, or "out of our depth".

Yet in making this element not for us, but beyond us, beneath us, and above us, an element where we are not at home, God has done something of great importance for us. He has provided us an escape from ourselves. And that, too, is an aspect of the beauty of the sea as we experience it. It is a space we may move into, never filled by our moving into it but forever uncolonised and free. It offers us an open door from the prisons we have built for ourselves. Running away to sea was traditionally the way the young escaped from their society and its controls, found their way out of the womb of expectations and predictions. In going to sea we cast ourselves on God's element that is not ours, place ourselves where we are not at home, and perhaps come to grips with the deepest spiritual questions about how we may be at home with ourselves. Jonah is the patron saint of all who have run to the sea to escape, because Jonah tried to flee from God there, and finally found him.

The moment of escape may be essential for us. Yet what that hard and demanding teacher tells us is that it cannot be the end of the story. We may *find* our freedom on the waves, but we cannot *live* our freedom out there, for freedom is brought to nothing through the inexorable struggle of the waves to encompass our destruction. Being at sea can only be an interval, a getaway break from walking on the land. From the first moment the merchant vessel casts off, the navigator plots its course for the port where it will tie up. Even the fisherman never sets out from harbour without a thought as to when and where he will land his catch.

Launched upon Life by God's Word

When God appointed the great fish to deliver Jonah onto dry land, he was only bringing him where his journey was bound to end anyway, unless, that is, he were to finish as food for a less accommodating species of fish. The sea is a teacher through whose class we must pass and then graduate. God has used the sea and its restlessness in many troubled and fugitive lives, but has used it to bring them to the point where they can find their rest in him, and be at home with themselves, on dry land.

He bringeth them unto the haven where they would be (Ps. 107:30). The object of a voyage is to reach port. The adventure is concluded as the sailor sets foot on the quay, hangs up his souwesters, and puts himself before the fireside. But coming home is a special relation with the land, a relation only the seafarer has in quite that form, since only the seafarer has laboured away from land. It is not those conventionally called "land-lubbers" who know how to love the dry land, but those who have learned from some hard and demanding maritime instruction that the land is their home. Yet *that* is a lesson that the sea alone cannot teach; it can only be the examiner. To learn it, we need another teacher.

The disciples struggled with the Sea of Galilee, and all their maritime skills were not enough, until he came to them who can find a place for the sole of his foot in everything that he has made. But then — and I wonder whether you noticed this as the story was read — *immediately the boat reached the land they were making for* (John 6:21). Only he could be as much at home on the waves as on dry land, for *the sea is his and he made it, and his hands prepared the dry land.* They could not be at home there. But when he came to them, they were at home, immediately. That is because *he* was their true home.

The most important thing in going to sea is that we should meet there the God who is the firm ground beneath our feet, our home. The seafarer who attains that has been a good student in the school of the sea; he has learned what the sea can teach, and more. But that seafarer is also a teacher of others, who can show the landlubber what it means that human life as such is a voyage, not a manufacturing operation, and that the point of casting off in freedom is to tie up in God's harbour.

How to Be a Human Being

Be fruitful and multiply, and fill the earth and subdue it.   GENESIS 1:28

You may say, "How to be a member of the human race is not something I need to learn. I *am* a member of the human race". And that is true. But suppose you were to start "playing God", as the mad scientists of fiction, fable, and sometimes, alas! fact are said to. Then you would need reminding, "*That's* not how a member of the human race behaves!" Or suppose that when you put down a bowl for your pets to feed from, you put down your own plate beside theirs and got down on all fours, snapping up your food with your teeth. Someone would have to tell you, "*That's* not how a member of the human race behaves. You're not a Pekinese! Learn *how to be* what you are!"

"Human" is something we cannot help being; but we can fail or succeed in being it. That is why the word "human" can sometimes mean "fallible", while the word "humanity" can be the name of a virtue. We can fail in being human because we don't understand what it is to be a human being. In *The Magic Flute* Sarastro sings: "whoe'er these truths will not maintain, doth not deserve to be a man". Being a man is something we must understand, in order to deserve to be it, even though it is what we are.

The first chapter of Genesis is written to instruct us. It is not a cosmological speculation but a moral lesson on how to be a member of the

3rd February 2002.

human race. The goal of its story is the sixth and seventh days, when Adam was created and God rested from his labours. But if the narrative has man as its climax, think how long it takes to get to him! Five days of creation in which nothing human shows its face! The earth was long in waiting for our kind, yet never idle. Five days of creation in which God finds it good! We were not needed for the goodness of planets and stars, of vegetation and animals. They were good on their own terms, or rather their Creator's terms, not needing you or me to find them so. Have you ever been tempted to think that the meaning of the word "good" was "what we want" or "what suits us"? Like Cleanthes the Stoic, who said that pigs are simply meals on four legs? If so, you haven't learned how to be a member of the human race. Your imagination has not stretched to encompass the objectivity of the universe apart from and before the human race. You have not learned that what came before us, all the energy and life that teemed across the vast spaces of the universe and planet, and still teems, was simply good.

So the first lesson in how to be a human being is to know that there are other kinds of things. We are surrounded by things not *quite* like us, by things *not at all* like us, and by things *very unlike* us. All of them good, all of them different, all but a few pets wholly careless of what we think of them, all God's handiwork in which he takes satisfaction!

One of the intellectual perils in the knowledge of genetic and evolutionary causality is forgetfulness of difference. "Everything is what it is, and not some other thing", Bishop Butler famously said. But that is what we are no longer sure of. Everything appears to be some other thing. With Darwin the difference of the human species was lost sight of; what were we, after all, but one pool of interbreeding mammals who had lost our capacity to breed with collaterals? With the uncoding of DNA, the difference of the living organism was lost sight of as well. How can we maintain difference between kind and kind, between one thing and another thing? How can we think of ourselves as humans and our pets as cats and dogs, when we are all just moments in the flow of biological life? We can do so by acknowledging their goodness. It is the final cause that makes the kind. By valuing each thing for what it is, we recognise it for what it is and not some other thing.

The story of creation reaches its climax. Mankind is created in God's image, male and female, and given dominion over the rest of creation.

Not that creation exists only *for* man; it exists for God, and for itself. But humanity brings something extra to creation, brings it to a fulfilment that it could not otherwise have, and this is human "dominion". Talk of "dominion" has sometimes been misunderstood to justify irresponsible exploitation. But it is not *dominion* that we consume animals and vegetables. That is simply our mode of conforming to the universal law on which all life is constructed, namely, that it nourishes itself on other life. What makes for dominion is that we can understand and interpret.

Our human privilege is that of knowing. We can observe the universe of creatures that do not exist for us, that are not just a "standing reserve", in Heidegger's memorable expression, a sinking fund with no designation existing only to support whatever we happen to have in mind. Our human privilege is to conduct ourselves appropriately in such a universe, using the control that knowledge gives to secure a context not only favourable to ourselves but to the variety of creatures God has made. The stabilising of the ecosystem is the lordly task set before the human race. To speak of "stewardship" of creation is helpful; it suggests our responsibility, even for the rats. It is not helpful, I think, to speak of the rats as our "brothers and sisters". We shall not learn responsibility for them by thinking of them that way any more than by thinking of them simply as pests.

It is no more paradoxical to think that human beings have a special dignity than to think that animals have a special dignity. All vegetarians, I suppose, think that animal life is special in a way that plant life is not. To deny any order of dignity among living things is not a recipe for vegetarianism, but for cannibalism. Plants, too, deserve their meed of respect; so do micro-organisms, and so, even, do inanimate things. We should think twice before ripping a healthy rosebush out or dynamiting a road through a mountain. Yet we need not feel unduly guilty about weeding or clearing stones off the lawn. Nor, so far as I can see, should we feel guilty about eating pork. You can tell I am unsympathetic to vegetarianism; but if you are a vegetarian, there is some comfort for you in Genesis: in the paradisal state, it thinks, Adam and Eve had a vegetarian diet, and only the harsh realities of a disordered universe required the disciplined and respectful use of meat. On the need for discipline and respect, at any rate, we ought to agree. A pig is not a meal on four legs, even if we sometimes make a meal of a pig. On any account the condi-

Launched upon Life by God's Word

tions in which some creatures God has made are bred for food are a disgrace to civilisation.

The dignity of mankind, for Genesis, rests on this: it is to humans, male and female, that God speaks in the second person: *"Be fruitful and multiply, and fill the earth and subdue it."* If there was some equivalent address to other forms of life, if they, too, can become "thou" to God, we are not privy to it; and we must guard ourselves, here as always, against what Barth called "the wanton play of the imagination". God's "Thou" is known to us only as we hear it addressed to us, holding us responsible to him. And in this relation of each of us to God, our relation to our own species is changed. We are no longer merely *instances* of *homo sapiens:* we are — as we say, for want of a better term — *persons.* To learn how to be a human being is to learn *personal existence,* hearing God's address to ourselves, answering God's summons for ourselves, being faithful to God's trust for ourselves. It is to learn to accept our life as given us by God.

Selling Possessions

"Sell your possessions, give to the poor, and you will
have treasure in heaven; then come and follow me."   MATTHEW 19:21

One thing that clearly doesn't trouble that ironic old observer known as "Preacher" or "Ecclesiastes" is simple plain consumption. If someone wants a meal and has the price in his pocket, he had better eat and drink. If someone can afford clothes to hang on his limbs, he had better dress himself. If someone needs a roof over his head, he had better buy a house if he can find the down payment. *It is a gift of God that every man to whom he has granted wealth and riches and the power to enjoy them should accept his lot and rejoice in his labour* (Eccl. 5:19). It's not in *that* department that the great mistakes are made. Yes, there are sins of the belly. We can eat and drink too much. But the belly is of finite dimensions, and sins against it are punished in the course of nature, whereupon we either learn from our discomfort or something else is wrong with us, something of an altogether greater order.

The problem arises with our appetite for what we can't consume but only accumulate: the clothes in our wardrobe that we do not wear, the books on our shelves that we do not consult, the CD's on the rack that we do not listen to — and the balance in our bank accounts that we do not spend. Two things go wrong here. One is the diversion of our efforts from worthwhile tasks to the mere protection of our wealth; the

21st September 1997.

other is the diversion of our appetites from worthwhile objects. I shall come back to the second shortly. For the moment, let us think about the first: how from productive and rewarding work we turn our attention to the fruitless and frustrating business of trying to maintain the current value of assets that we do not and will not use up. The bigger our store gets, the disproportionately greater effort it takes to service it. A few unused books can lie around without much looking after, but clothes need regular cleaning and protection from the moths, while stocks and shares seem to need incessant loving-care and attention. *Gnawing anxiety and great vexation are his lot,* declares the Preacher (Eccl. 5:17). One might be doing something much more rewarding. I often think of the theologian who, as wicked rumour had it, rushed to the bank on the morning after Labour won the General Election of 1964, and converted his life's savings into dollars in anticipation of devaluation. What careful forethought! What planning! What hours spent poring over the financial columns of the papers! What might we have had, what might he have done, if those hours, that energy, that focussed thought, had been given to . . . theology!

For there is a kind of law of entropy affecting all accumulated wealth, which constantly overwhelms our attempts to appropriate what we think of as our property. *When riches multiply, so do those who live off them; and what advantage has the owner then, except to look at them?* (Eccl. 5:11). That is not a moral comment, but merely an observation on one of those premoral laws by which divine providence governs the relation of a society to its material resources. We heard the story on the news this week of how a massive criminal syndicate has cashed in worldwide upon pirated CD's. Without saying a word to excuse it, we may be allowed to think that it is, after all, a very predictable result of preposterous concentrations of wealth in the pop-music CD business. It is tempting to think that Oasis will hardly notice their loss. Wealth attracts parasites as dung attracts beetles; it's a law of life. The curious thing is that so much of the time it happens in a semi-institutionalised manner, with the collusion of the owner. The gnawing anxiety and great vexation of maintaining the value of an asset can be such that one will sometimes prefer to be stripped of it within a system of symbolic exchanges, rewarded for one's passivity with an elegant but empty deference. Where would our Directors of Development be otherwise? By such means

Providence ensures that those who have wealth can be rid of it as quickly and pleasantly as possible. Some wit, as I remember, christened the National Lottery "a tax on the daft". And taxes on the daft of one kind or another are known in every description of society.

With which we come to the tax collector. For our excuse for these reflections is the happy occurrence of St. Matthew's Day on a Sunday. There are, of course, two St. Matthews, who may, after all, be one and the same person but even so invite different lines of thought. There is Matthew the author of the first Gospel, the rabbinic student who found in Jesus' teaching the conclusive exposition of the Law of God for which Israel had been seeking. And there is Levi-Matthew the tax collector, who abandoned his administrative responsibilities to be one of the twelve and proclaim the Kingdom of God. Our lectionary, with its two magnificent readings on the futility of accumulated wealth, has pointed us to Levi this morning. But what precisely is the connexion that it has in mind? Is Levi before he met with Jesus supposed to have been the type of the greedy and acquisitive man, like that other tax collector in the Gospels, Zacchaeus, who climbed a tree and promised to restore fourfold what he had cheated anyone of? Tax collectors had a bad reputation as a class; but we know nothing against Levi on this score. But tax collectors were also resented for their connexion with an alien and imposed government, whose levying of taxes was controversial and resisted. And as such Levi represents a law of Providence, a paradoxical contradiction that lurks inescapably at the very heart of the idea of private wealth. What I own is not my own. Where I appropriate I am most subject to forces that alienate. Taxation is simply the most formal and institutional demonstration that property and alienation always make their appearance together.

I mentioned a second thing that goes wrong with accumulated wealth. Not only is our property subject to a law of alienation; our imaginations and purposes also become alienated. Our efforts are diverted to securing the value of what we own, and so our appetites are diverted from pursuing something to pursuing nothing. For wealth does not exist as such. Money exists; it is a means of exchange and a symbolic form of power to act in certain ways in social contexts. We can perfectly sensibly want the power that money confers, *in order to do something with it.* If you are beginning to think that the drift of my remarks has been hostile to saving or to common prudence, let me reassure you. By all means let us save — for this or for that good undertaking! By all means let us collect money, to found a business or a charitable enterprise, or, for private purposes, to buy ourselves a home or to provide for our retirement, to insure ourselves against long illness or our family against our sudden deaths! Not everything, of course, that we might want to do with our money would be good to do; and not everything that might be good to do in principle will be given to us to do in fact, for any individual person can only do so many things in the scope of one life. Nevertheless, we are put in this world to do things, and as we discern what we are to do, so we discern a good reason to save up to do it. But prudence, let me remind you, is the virtue of selecting appropriate means to appropriate ends. The problem comes when we save up without an end, "for a rainy day" as we say, meaning for nothing whatever in particular. At that point our practical imaginations have lost their hold on the good ends given us to pursue, our appetites have fallen back to wallow in mere means, which cannot even be means in the proper sense at all, since they have no ends to serve. To love riches is to love an empty abstraction, an image of our own power; and this image becomes a substitute for the real things we might have devoted our power to. Inevitably the love of wealth is addictive. It arises out of moral and imaginative exhaustion, when we can't find anything good to do; and it conceals that exhaustion from us with the illusion that we are devoting our energies to a purpose.

Which brings us to the point the Preacher thinks of as decisive. The key to avoiding the traps of wealth is to work. We may take a satisfaction in our work which we shall never be able to take in our wealth. The wealthy, too, may be content in this work, but that is because they are only incidentally wealthy, and the real determinant of their life is the labour they undertake. Let us explore this thought a little further. What is the difference between *gnawing anxiety* and *rejoicing in one's labour?*

Imagine you own five houses in different parts of the world. I can easily think of five houses in different parts of the world that I would love to own; but the idea of actually owning five houses at one time is little short of nightmarish. All your energy would be given to maintaining them and perhaps letting them, making sure they were clean, in good repair, not burgled, and that house-agents in different countries, writing in different languages and operating with different tax laws, were not cheating you. You wouldn't have time for anything else. But suppose you said to yourself, "There is nothing else that I do so well as I do this. I have acquired some skills and become something of an expert in the business, and I find my imagination and inventiveness stretched by the complex tasks involved in making those houses pleasant and safe for tenants to occupy". Then you might begin to regard this burden of maintaining your assets as a work in which you could take a genuine satisfaction. What is it that makes the qualitative difference? Is it simply a matter of internal attitude, the fact that you have, as it were, changed the look on your face from a scowl to a smile? No: a very important new factor has entered into the logic of what you are doing. It is *the tenants.* You are beginning to do what you do not for yourself but for them. You are taking satisfaction in getting things the way they will want them. It is work, now, because its goal is to provide something other people need. The difference between possessing and working lies not in the effort that each requires, but in the way that effort is directed outwards into society.

When you direct the effort you expend on your property outwards, you begin to "own" that property in a way you never did before. We own a thing not by consuming it, but by acting with it. It is ours only as it becomes *our contribution,* the vehicle of our engagement with society, as it takes on the stamp of our constructive purposes towards other people. Without that handing-over, without our possession becoming someone else's resource, it has never fully been ours, since it has never enabled us to *act,* which is to be ourselves. For the law of society is a law of communications; things are passed from one person to the next, changed and enriched by each person's creativity as they are so. What it means to have owned something is to have made it one's own communication to another.

Sell your possessions and give to the poor! Now, indeed, we are in a position to hear Jesus' words to the rich young man. For, you see, having made the transition in thought from owning to working, we have also made the transition from owning to giving. What makes owning fruitful is the work it enables. And what makes work fruitful is the need it discerns and addresses. All work is giving. All owning is selling, *i.e.* the realisation of possession as power.

Taken in their strictest sense, of course, Jesus' words apply only to the rich man and those like him who are in a position, and have a calling,

Launched upon Life by God's Word

to join a community with a common life and a common purse. But behind them is a logic that applies across the board, the logic of self-dispossession, the conversion of possession into gift. There is no other way; what I have must be given. All I have acquired of the resources for life are destined to this act of communication, whatever form it may take, by which another will receive from me and live. It is the work of my life to conceive and to carry through such acts of communication. And we may well pray that when our life ends, the work will be, if not completed, at least well begun, and that our bank accounts will not bear witness to powers we never used, opportunities we never took.

Levi the tax collector represents the law of Providence: what we claim as our own cannot be our own, but must become another's. But when he leaves his office to follow Jesus, the first thing he is recorded as doing, the only thing indeed, is to host an entertainment for Jesus and his friends. Levi the apostle represents the law of grace: what we extend in generosity to others creates a community that is really ours. For to give is to enter into community, to communicate *with*. And that is why the church asks us in one form or another to share our resources with it. It does so not just an apologetic afterthought, but as part of its invitation to us to hear and believe the gospel. To be a Christian is to be part of a community of giving and receiving, a community of poor and a community of rich, a community of need acknowledged and a community whose needs are met, a community founded by that great original gift of self, God's own self-communication to us in his Son. The young man is told: *You will have treasure in heaven.* To be part of *that* giving and receiving is to anticipate the eternal community of mankind with God.

Possessing Wisdom

*Happy is the man who finds wisdom, and the man
who gets understanding.*   PROVERBS 3:13

So wisdom is a possession, is it? Something to be found, something to
be got? An acquisition of more value than silver and gold, more precious
than jewels? A possession is something we have under our control,
something called on when we need it, a resource for meeting challenges
and opportunities. A possession is something we can exploit, deriving
other good things from it, such as long life, riches, honour, and peace. A
possession is a fragment of the world to which we relate by commanding it, appropriating it, taking it over. If wisdom is a possession, it must
be the supreme possession, the possession that contains all other possessions in itself, for wisdom is a relation not to a fragment of the world
but to the world as a whole, a grasp of its interrelations and connexions,
a comprehensive view. And since we ourselves are part of this world,
wisdom is also *self-possession,* the knowledge of our own place in that
complex of relations and connexions, allowing us to position ourselves
and to direct our lives. "Happy" the man who finds wisdom, declares
our poem. Such a one *makes a success of life,* we might say.

"Happy"! And since control and self-possession are attributes of
God, to be happy is to be godlike. At the conclusion of the poem we hear
that *the Lord by wisdom founded the earth.* The commanding relation of

---

9th October 2005, at the beginning of the University year.

Launched upon Life by God's Word

the Creator to the world is mirrored in the way the wise grasp hold of the world, which stands, as it were, at their beck and call.

Is it in the power of the University to confer wisdom? To judge by the sales talk emanating from the Student Access offices of our Universities these days, there can be no doubt about it! Three brief years of apprenticeship, plentifully interspersed with fashionable parties, and then. . . . what salaries shall we not command? What positions of power shall we not be appointed to? What achievements in the arts and sciences, in diplomacy and industry, shall we not find waiting to be accomplished, as we hurtle into life with the kinetic energy of a University degree? Yet we cannot suppress a suspicion that godlikeness is more elusive, harder to lay hold of. That the knowledge involved exceeds the requirements of any syllabus, that the apprenticeship will outlast the statutory three — "or", as a certain educational council likes to add in parentheses, "at the most, four" — years.

Glancing back at the third chapter of the Book of Proverbs, we notice that the passage in praise of wisdom began at the thirteenth verse. That is to say, it is the *second* stanza of a poem, not the first. And as one should never read the first lines of a poem without the conclusion, so one should never read the end of a poem without the beginning. Let us pick up where we should have begun, then. Immediately we notice a difference of mood, a difference, even, of vocabulary. The word "understanding" occurs not at all in the first stanza, the word "wisdom" only in the course of a warning not to presume on it: *be not wise in your own eyes.* Insight, another frequent synonym in Wisdom literature, is, we are told, not to be relied on. The expansive promises are still there, however: long life, economic welfare, good reputation, even health of body and mind, desirable acquisitions still but with the price quoted in a different currency. We are told of "discipline", "instruction", even "commands". We find ourselves bidden to accept what others tell us rather than calling on resources we were supposed to find within ourselves: *My son, do not forget my teaching!* We find ourselves expected to be deferential where we planned to be self-confident: *Do not despise the Lord's discipline!* God is still in view, and God is still decisive for the relation we are to have to the world. But where we were going to be godlike and to imitate the sovereign command with which the Most High surveys all things, we are told instead to be *trusting,* which means, not to put too fine a point on it, dependent.

Life itself is spoken of in different terms, as we can see from how the metaphor of life as a *way,* or *path,* is handled. The second stanza told us that the ways of wisdom are ways of pleasantness, and her paths are paths of peace, which looks like an attractive stroll along a pleasantly mown, carefully rolled path across the lawn, such as every English country house affords for a quick tour of the borders and shrubberies. The end of this pleasant path is the tree of life — and we all know which garden *that* tree stands in the centre of! But in the first stanza life's "ways" look and feel rather different. *In all your ways acknowledge him:* these are *our* ways, for one thing, not wisdom's. We have to cut back the branches and the nettles ourselves, since no one has ever taken this path before us, no one has lived the life which we have to live. *And he will make straight your paths,* for unless they are straightened out, we are at risk of losing our way.

The University, too, after all its expansive promises, may confront the one who enters it in just such a daunting and demanding tone of voice. Freshmen's fairs and college mothers-and-fathers make incoming undergraduates of this generation feel cozy and at home from the moment they step in, but my generation of students forty years ago found it not at all cozy to come to this place, and I would guess that even now the young have their moments of fear and trembling. You don't know what is expected of you; you want to succeed but don't know what success consists in; you are wholly dependent on direction, and yet with no assurance that even if you do exactly what you are told, or *think* you have been told, the class list at the end of it all will read satisfactorily. Neither University nor life itself is like A-levels, with their neat lists of points to memorise and mention.

So there, in two stanzas, we have two contrasted views of a life of wisdom. In one of them wisdom is possessed, in the other it is not possessed and cannot be, but must be sought out in the dark, under guidance and direction. And which is the true picture? Both are. Or, rather, they are true together, juxtaposed, set one beside the other.

Let us speak first of the point they have in common. The project of human life involves knowledge. With this we touch on what is most distinctive in the human relation to the world. All living beings exist in the world by consuming, by consuming other beings, in fact, many of those living beings, too. All animals exist in the world by moving through it in pursuit of their projects. But only human animals exist by knowing that they consume and knowing that they pursue. Only human animals can hold up their existence before their own eyes to form a view of their position in the whole. And if there are other creatures in the Universe that do so, they are like humans in this all-important respect. Only humans ask, "What are we here for?" Only humans put the question of God, the source and end, the where-from and where-to of existence. Only humans think about what it means to be happy, about what makes a success of life, and what a failure. Is life, then, a gigantic unrepeatable experiment, that may work or fail to work? Inescapably so, for us humans at least! And to say as much is to take the first tentative steps towards the vast task, of which only human beings are capable, of knowing ourselves. But precisely because we *can* make this beginning, we can explore the University not simply in terms of its expansive promises, not simply in terms of its daunting demands, but in pursuit of an answer to a question of our own, a question that overrides in its importance the promises and demands. Is the knowledge that the University offers apt to assist us in the human task we have taken up and can never put down, the task of knowing ourselves? Will it contribute to our wisdom?

Now, any sensible talk about wisdom has to take *beginnings* and *endings* into account. That is why there are two stanzas in the poem. The beginning is different from the end: wisdom "begins" in non-possession, in a dependent posture of trust and obedience, and "ends" in the security of possession. But what beginnings and what endings are these? It may seem at the University that life begins in terror and ends in triumph, the freshman students nervous and uncertain, the dons complacent and self-satisfied. But it is not really like that, not even here, and certainly not in life itself. It is not youth that consists of terror, age of triumph. Youth has its glory, of which age must stand in envy. And there is no more terrifying challenge, no part of life where we are more totally bereft of understanding and thrust back upon trust, than age's last and most decisive examination, death, when the blood fails to reach the brain and all the Portuguese irregular verbs we ever learned cease to be at our command, when all we have relied on, all we have been filled with, is drained out of us. If wisdom can be possessed in the end, it can only be an end *beyond* that utter dispossession. But then we shall need, not less but more than ever, an orientation to our state which is given us in knowledge. For what we can still know when we no longer know anything else, the knowledge that will serve us when all knowledge else is vain, is knowledge indeed, knowledge that confers life, even life in death.

It does not yet appear what we shall be, we read in the chapter from the First Letter of John this morning; *but we know that when he appears, we shall be like him.* The end, again, consists in godlikeness. But this end is not our natural end, but lies beyond our end. It is the appearing of God that will bring our wisdom to its goal and make our likeness to him possible. Until God shows himself face to face, all the godlikeness we aspire to is no more than a fragment, perilous in its partiality and incompleteness. I hardly need to insist on the dangers of aspiring to godlikeness in terms of power without goodness, the concentration on technology with its capacity to destroy and transform the world and its order. That is merely the showcase in which the dangers of our knowing are displayed to us. All our knowledge and wisdom, in fact, even the most contemplative and philosophical, the most philanthropic and benign, have lurking within them destructive possibilities of contempt and despair. For in reaching out for wisdom we reach out to encompass what will always escape us, a whole that is always partial, a sun that is always in eclipse. But, the apostle assures us, God *will* appear; and then we shall find the wisdom that our restless striving after knowledge promises and denies us.

And what in the meantime? Is there nothing more than doubt and blind risk? Nothing more than sceptical adherence to tradition for want of any other guide? Critiques with nothing left that is worth critiquing? Rules of intellectual discipline for discipline's sake? There is more. From the beginning we have what the apostle calls a "message": *this is the message that you have heard from the beginning, that we should love one another.* If we *must* wait for God's appearing, the reason we *can* do so is that we have this token given us already. The Son of God has appeared *to destroy the works of the devil,* to put that wonderful co-involvement of trust between human and human, the *love of the brethren,* in place of doubt and distrust.

So to the most important question: can a University teach us love of the brethren? Can it impart a joy in others' existence, a passion for relations that determine and construct identities? A University is a much

Launched upon Life by God's Word

bigger place, and a much more complex interaction, than the Administration is likely to be aware of. Its operations stretch more widely than the lecture lists and library catalogues. The influence that its members have on one another works more profoundly than the formal lessons they teach and learn. Perhaps almost all the formal knowledge we acquire will be no more than data-gathering, from which we shall have to filter out the real knowledge, the knowledge that will serve us in good stead finally and supremely in death, the knowledge that we must fear the Lord, turn away from evil, and not despise his discipline. But if, while we are looking out for what the University teaches, we are prepared for it to teach us this too, then in the grace of God I believe it can do so, and all its other teaching then takes on a higher significance. Not only the trappings of wisdom but its heart may be encountered here, if we are ready to seek and find, and not to despise the Lord's discipline.

The Honour of Marriage

Let marriage be held in honour among all. HEBREWS 13:4

What the apostle was on guard against in pleading for the "honour" of marriage was an overenthusiastic championing of the single life, disapproving of the married state. In our current circumstances, however, we face the question of how to honour marriage in quite different terms. Twice in recent months the House of Bishops has addressed the Church on marriage. In January it was a working party report proposing pastoral guidelines for the marriage in church of divorced people with previous partners still living; four months earlier, to prepare the way for those proposals, the bishops published a shorter piece of their own, restating the Church's doctrine of marriage and addressing it to current problems.

The marriage-breakdown situation is surely one of the most serious challenges to the integrity of the Christian church at the moment, far more serious than many others which excite a great deal more noise. And it would seem to be something of an epidemic. Couples are divorcing in part just because other couples have divorced, for in matters of the emotions we all learn by example. And now a new problem has been generated, which is the sheer unwillingness of young couples to get married any more. And who can be surprised at that? A young man and woman involved in a serious attachment, which would in another age

2nd April 2000, in Southwell Minster.

Launched upon Life by God's Word

have become a marriage without much fuss, look round on siblings divorced, parents estranged, and may, perhaps, have no experience to look back on of being brought up by two married parents. Can we wonder if their hearts fail them? How can I promise to be a faithful wife, when faithfulness in intimate relations is something I have never observed close up? How can I contemplate being a father when I have never had a father in my home?

Young people are, indeed, the great losers in the present situation, but they are not the only losers. Friendship loses out, too, as congenial social ties are riven into splinters around a fractured marriage. But the worst sufferers are the couples themselves, especially later, when they grow old. The bishops make a telling observation on the phrase "till death us do part": "Knowing that they must both one day die", they say, "the partners offer each other a security and continuity in life that will help them approach death with humility and good conscience". The distinctive contribution of marriage to our welfare, they tell us, is that it helps us approach death. The continuity of married life stretching over the years provides a thread around which we may assemble our memories, come to terms with what we have been and done, and find peace. But the memories we need are the memories we have had to suppress in order to cope with the disruption of a broken marriage. If they come back, it may be in a demonic form, unintegrated, obsessive, not woven into the fabric of our lives. It is a painful thing when old to be haunted by wrongs one has not forgiven and by pain one has not assuaged, when all the other actors are dead and there is no one at hand to help us to forgive.

Marriage is a storm-tossed ship, in need of Christ's word to calm the waves that batter it. And the irony is that marriage itself was supposed to afford us calm. That calm, of course, has been much idealised. A landlubber who enjoys the sights and sounds of a harbour on a pleasant summer afternoon may find them soothing; but that has nothing to do with the experience of sailing. Once let him leave the shore, once let him hear the creaking of the boards and feel the lurching of the floor, and he may quickly conclude that his voyage will end in catastrophe. But in fact the motion and the straining are the very things that ensure stability, as the pressures of the waves are distributed through the structure of the vessel and the impact of each shock reduced to a fraction of its real force. So, too, the emotional tremors that run through a marriage may frighten us when we are new to the ship, especially if we have had no opportunity to learn how much rocking and bumping there can be in quite a comfortable relationship. But they are a sign that marriage is doing its job.

For marriage and family is where emotional ups and downs are expressed and stabilised. Triumph and loss, fear, frustration, and achievement, all take their paths through the family, and are woven there into the small details of ordinary life, absorbed into the round of eating, sleeping, and waking, making matter for laughter and consolation, scolding and argument. Their resonances pass from one member to another, making a framework of objectivity and support for the member most immediately affected. The hollow in the pit of the stomach of a child on the very first day of school gnaws at the vitals of the parents, too; and their reaction to the challenge is what gives the child courage. This is the service that a family renders all its members, children and adults alike — for we must avoid the trap of thinking that the family is "for" the children. We all need its help. Poor health and disappointment, excitement and delirious pleasure, all the emotional demands that life makes, spread through the family, diffused across a structure built by God to contain them and make them safe for us. In the family more than any other community we learn the truth of the saying, *If one member suffers, all suffer together. If one member is honoured all rejoice together.*

Yes, and the family must know anger. I would even say that the family is the natural home of anger, the one place where anger is safely expressed, accepted, turned aside, and dissipated, converted into hope and consolation. Of course, we know that there can be too much anger even for a family. The persistent bitterness of one member, particularly a parent, can inflict long-lasting harm on the others. But the fact that waves may rise so high as to sink a ship doesn't mean that ships are not built to withstand waves. The family can withstand anger, provided only that it is protected by constant mutual attentiveness, each member alert to the responses of the others. The attentiveness of love, which heeds the warning signals when one member can cope with anger no more, teaches us to moderate our anger and deflect it.

And at the centre of the family, the girder which holds the frame together, there is the marriage. And just as we must avoid thinking that the family is "for" the children, so we must avoid thinking that the marriage is "for" the couple. For while children need to be loved themselves, they also need the presence of the love of adults for each other. When they no longer stand in need of the cossetting that is the child's privilege, they will still need *that* love carrying on, as it were, behind their backs. What is it that is so special about that central relation, making it different from every other relation in the family? It spans the gulf between two kinds of love. It blends the love which ties us tightly to our own, which the Greeks called *storgê,* that identification most supremely expressed in the almost organic unity of a mother and her baby, together with the love that reaches out in fascination for the distant and the different, the love called *eros.* Familial love is *storgê,* identification, defensive and possessive — which is why parents so often behave badly at parent-teacher meetings! But in the love of husband and wife this is blended with a strand of wonder and amazement, the discovery of the self in the different, "mine own and not mine own". And the presence of *that* love in the family is like air in the soil; it allows the other love to be nourishing, not suffocating. It says to the children: you *may* leave home, and the love of your home will not be destroyed when you go out to find another love. But it also says: when you find the new horizon of that other love opening up before you in wonder, you will be brought back through that wonder into the stable and familiar love of a home. A generation brought up without two parents will be a generation that finds it difficult to make *eros* and *storgê* blend. For them love will present itself as a dangerous either-or, either the wild adventure or the sense of homely security, the two never fusing into one.

Marriage is at the heart of the family, the family at the heart of our social interactions. And this position, which makes it so important, also makes it vulnerable. There are many reasons why marriages break down, and any attempt to find a single universal cause is ridiculous; but one recurrent element is the scapegoat factor. It is a cruel extension of that proper exchange of burdens that occurs in marriage. My partner bears the blame for my despair with myself, whatever may be its cause, and so my partner becomes the sacrifice required by my need to reinvent myself. I think of a clergyman with four happy children, whose family life was conducted in that kind of relaxed and exuberant style which results in the visitor's being hit by a pillow on entering the front hall. Like many clergymen, this one worked from home, and inevitably his study became a permanent extension of the children's playground. As he entered that long stretch of life so dangerous for men, when youthful promotion has come to an end and what they are is what they are going to be, he was visited by old regrets from student days about his second-class scholastic accomplishments. Quite suddenly one day he walked out of his rectory and out of his family to enroll somewhere in a programme of graduate study. It seemed as clear as day to his friends that the point of this traumatic self-reinvention was to find some space to concentrate. It was his children he wanted to divorce. But he could not say that, to himself or to anyone, and the only acceptable account of his problem was that he couldn't get on with his wife.

Are you bound to a wife? Do not seek to be free. Are you free from a wife? Do not seek marriage. Such was Saint Paul's "advice" — he himself would not call it by any stronger word. *Do not seek to be free,* is the more obvious bit. For marriage embodies the paradox of freedom, that to be free we must be bound. Freedom is enacted in the cancellation of open possibilities; it is focussed in the moment when we say, "I will". When we have said it, our freedom is proved by the fact that the other possibilities are no longer open. We have actualised the possibility of marriage, and so bound ourselves. If we seek to be free *to marry,* just as we were free before, all we really want is impotence, to have the appearance of marrying without the real effects of marriage. Freedom *in* marriage is not the same as that earlier freedom *to* marry; it is a freedom for other things, the things that marriage supports and makes possible.

But Paul's other piece of advice, *Do not seek marriage,* may be equally important, especially for the divorced. Now, I am among those who think that a divorced person may truly be called by God to marry again. But only single people can marry, and I am troubled when I see people hurrying into second marriages without first reaching the independence of singleness. This urgency owes too much to a need to overcome failure, or to a search for self-vindication. Those are dangerous dynamics, launching the new marriage on the swell thrown up by the foundering of the old. And they are the reason why the bishops wisely urge what are coming to be called the "three distances". A new marriage should be separated from the old by "distance of time, of local setting, and of relationship. Time is need to recover emotional stability and good judgment; a new setting is needed, in which the former partner is not forced to endure the reopening of old wounds; and a new relationship is needed, avoiding suspicion that the new marriage consecrates old infidelity".

Paul himself made an exception to the advice, *Do not seek marriage!* though his words have rung so strangely in modern ears that he doesn't get much credit for their common sense. The young unmarried, for whom it is the natural instinct of their development to yearn for a partner and to start a family, are in a case of their own. But these are the very ones who today most shrink from marriage. Ready to risk themselves to the extent of sharing a home, they find it almost insuperably difficult to make a promise for life. One shouldn't have to tell the young to marry. One should only have to tell them to be cautious and careful and take plenty of time, and all the other things that have been repeated from time immemorial and to so little effect. That advice is still relevant; but now they also need a word to encourage them forwards.

Shall we frame that word something like this? "The problems that will confront you are not so much problems of marriage as problems of life — problems, in particular, of *your* lives, which you are bound to confront in some context and in some way, regardless of whether you marry or not. You will grow bored with being young. You will find your ambitions and what you expect from life changing. You will want what you do not now want, you will not want what you want now. You will have the normal worries about money and status and achievement. You will have disappointments as well as triumphs. You will find your physical strength growing less, and in time you must expect to suffer the indignities of old age and death. The question is, are you called by God to live through these things *together*? If not, you had better split up at once, for with every day you stay together, emotional independence retreats further out of reach. But if you are, you should equip yourselves with the structures of public promise and private pledge, of firm expectation and settled role, that will help you stay the course. Where is your faith? The winds and waves have sunk many thoughtless and ill-prepared seafarers, it is true. But the ship of marriage is well built, and the shipbuilder himself is ready to make the voyage with you as your passenger."

Looking Forward

Forgetting what lies behind and straining forward
to what lies ahead . . .   PHILIPPIANS 3:13

It seems to us, as we embark on Paul's memorable description of the change of values that transformed his life, that we can see fairly clearly where it is going. Taking off from a dismissive and impatient reference to a group of religious enthusiasts with a bent for ritual — *the circumcision party* — Paul recounts how he learned not to value external ritual and legal formality, *the flesh,* of which circumcision is the paradigm, but came to value something else more highly. This other thing is variously described as the knowledge of Christ, the power of Christ's resurrection, worship in the spirit, and the righteousness of faith. The whole account refers, evidently enough, to the encounter with Christ on the Damascus road, so we take it as a before-and-after story, a narrative that contrasts Paul's values on either side of that dramatic reversal.

One or two ripples on the surface of the narrative may possibly disturb us. *Righteousness by faith in Christ* is contrasted with what he calls *my own righteousness of the law.* In what way, we may wonder, is righteousness by faith *not* his own, if it is the supreme value of his new life? And then there is the shift of tense from past, *I suffered the loss of all things,* to present, *and count them as refuse . . . that I may gain Christ,* as though he were taking himself back in his imagination to the very mo-

---

23rd March 2003.

Launched upon Life by God's Word

ment of his change of heart. What has become of the twenty years or so of faithful service to the spiritual ideal, the years which separate the Damascus road from the time of Paul's writing to the Philippians? Why have these vanished from the narrative?

Then we read the words, *Not that I have already obtained this . . . but I am in pursuit of it.* It is one of those moments at which a text seems to undergo a kaleidoscopic shift. It is like one of those peremptory key-changes with which Mozart introduces the development section of a sonata movement. We realise that we didn't understand where Paul was heading at all. The transition from flesh to spirit was not a change of values; it was a change in the whole relation in which he stood *to* values. *The flesh* was not just outward ritual; it was self-valuation of every kind. To worship in the spirit is to give up making the self the object of conscientious attention. The self is no longer the route to the goal. The event Paul describes was not one in which he *grasped* a thing of value; it was, he tells us, an event in which he *was grasped,* leaving him with a task of grasping that he has pursued unfinished ever since. Now we see why the twenty years are missing from the narrative. They have contributed nothing to Paul's quest. *Forgetting what lies behind, straining forward to what lies ahead,* all that he has been and done, since his conversion as well as before it, disappears from sight.

Let us make four observations on this change from flesh to spirit.

First, it is a change in the way we think about our active lives, no longer oriented round the self, but oriented to something from outside the self, the *upward call,* as he puts it. It takes us out of a primarily reflective into a primarily deliberative mode of thinking, stressing the forward-looking nature of the active posture. Yet perhaps this raises a doubt in our minds. Does it not undermine the important moral duty of consistency? Does it not encourage us to reinvent ourselves every day, to have no stability of purpose or character? If there is one theme that has dominated moral philosophy in the last generation, it has been consistency of character. The moral self, it is claimed, is a situated and determined self, a self with a narrative history. But Paul seems to be recommending an undetermined self. This discounting of coherence over time — is it not morally nihilistic? No, it is not. For the question about consistency is always, consistency *with what?* We do not achieve *moral* consistency simply by measuring ourselves against our own idea of ourself. Consistency with oneself is an aesthetic posture, not a moral one. King David, the story goes, more used to marching out at the head of his troops in battle array, scandalised his wife and earned the sharp edge of her tongue by dancing in public in nothing but a loincloth when the ark of the Lord was ceremoniously brought into Jerusalem. And the Lord punished David's wife for her scorn by making her barren. Which is an allegory: a role-bound behavioural consistency is morally unfruitful. The pagan ethic of honour is concerned with what is due to our own position. True moral consistency is concerned with what is due to God, and that allows and requires a constantly *new* discernment of God's purposes. There is a paradox here, of course. Paul has contrasted the righteousness of faith with the righteousness of the law. But by that he means the righteousness of *institutionalised* law, the Mosaic order. *Divine* law is more flexible, more free, more constructive, precisely because the will of God is always old and always new, maintaining continuity through every difference of circumstance.

Are we to say, then, that the important thing is ethics, not doctrine, practical reason not theoretical reason? Are we to go back to the old slogans of muscular Christianity, "doctrine divides, service unites", and tell ourselves to roll our sleeves up? No, because those slogans, too, bring *preconceptions* to bear upon the upward call of God in Christ Jesus. They have programmes already made, agendas prepared to roll out. "Ethics", in one sense of the word, is part of the problem for Paul, to the extent that Ethics is programme-driven. What he is urging on us is a posture of *practical discernment*.

What, secondly, must we think about the moral significance of *memory?* On the face of it Paul is simply opposed to remembering: "forgetting what is behind. . . ." But in fact, of course, Paul never stopped remembering. The whole of this passage, like so much else that he wrote, springs from that infinitely fruitful focus of his memory, the event on the Damascus road. So the question is not whether to remember, but how to. Memory, like every other movement of the mind, has to serve the upward call. It has to prepare us to recognise that moment, not shield us against it. There must be a "transition", a "crossing over" from the receipt of the past to embarking on the future, a moment of true "present", where past and future form the horizons on one side and the other. This moment occurs precisely as the past becomes memory. For that is what frees us from always re-living, re-enacting, re-embarking on what is over and done with. To remember constructively is, in one sense, to disown the past, not in the sense of denying it, but gaining a distance on it, *discounting it,* in Paul's metaphor, against the gain that is offered us on the other horizon. And how do we discount it? By setting it to God's account. That is why we are so often told by the apostles to give thanks. Thankful memory transfers events out of our own field of action into the record of God's deeds for us. Our past becomes transparent to him and to his works. Whatever your mind may be stocked with, Paul says to his readers, God will require you to add this measure of distance, too; no memory, whether of good or ill, can be good *for* us, until we have made it over to him by thanksgiving, and so freed ourselves from its hold.

If there is a need for distance on the past, in the third place, how can it be different with the future? Intent on what lies before us, the essential thing is to confront the future *as our horizon,* the possibility that is open to our present moment. We cannot grasp the future. The future is not available to us to recount, as the past is. It is undetermined, unknown, and unrealised. The future is wholly God's. So to face the future is to face a giddy void, to be like someone suddenly seized by vertigo on a cliff-edge in swirling mist. To avoid this we will go to any lengths to grasp imaginary futures that are not real at all. Our imagination supplies us with endless different futures to suit our moods: a future of cherished plans and ambitions, a speculative future governed by a Big Idea, a future of extrapolated trends, safely predictable, a future of disaster embodying all our fears. All these are somehow easier to deal with than the future of God's planning, which we can only receive from God as and when he is ready to show it to us. What we need, then, is not clear ideas about the future — God forbid! they are the *worst* things we could have! — but a constant and wholly realistic attentiveness, a readiness to see what God is sending and how he is sending it, as when we strain our eyes to the horizon to be sure to see at once when something awaited appears like a speck. This is a habit of soul that we can cultivate from small things to great, from the ring of a doorbell to the consequences of a war, praying each day to be granted to recognise, not to overlook, not to walk past, the place where God is calling us upwards.

It is said often, but deserves saying: knowing Christ is not like knowing *something*, but like knowing *someone*. I cannot imagine what it would be like to know the solution to Fermat's last theorem, let alone discover it. But once Sir Andrew Wiles did discover it, when the loose ends were finally in place and the doubts resolved, I imagine that he simply *knew* it, and that was that. He could recount, publicise, and explain; or he could take up new projects that arose out of it. But the solution of the theorem was done, it was memory. Quite different is the knowledge we have of people. Until they die that knowledge never moves onto the past horizon, but is always on the future horizon, still opening out. In marriage we have an image of the perpetual attentiveness required of us in relation to God's call. We are always waiting on each other: what will she do or say next? What astonishing thing am I about to witness?

My fourth observation is addressed to the condition of some of us. I have never been too enamoured of Gregory the Great's advice that preachers should speak to the condition of their hearers, but with this text before us, I cannot close without drawing out a lesson that seems especially intended for those who are mature in their development. In this place I can usually be certain of hearers who, like myself, have the longer part of their lives behind them, those whose broad lines of personality, habit, achievement are long since settled. Paul speaks directly to us, when he articulates a paradox about maturity: *It is not as though I had attained, or were mature. . . . As many of you as are mature, have this in your mind.* The sign of spiritual maturity is to have a continuing sense of one's own immaturity. For whatever else our mind contains — whatever stock of memory, principle, accomplishment — God will require us to add this, too: a recognition of our own incompleteness as a human being, the attention to the task still before us.

Do we think our life is past, our work done? Then we must reckon with that sphinx-like apophthegm with which Paul closes: *wherever you may have arrived, walk there!* Arriving at the place we were headed for is not, it seems, the nub of the matter; it remains to "walk there", reaping the fruits of our journey. It is as though the whole course through life so far had been by aeroplane and bus, and only now does the serious question arise whether we have any spiritual leg muscles fit for use on our own account.

When we were younger, our minds were set on getting there, on the next promotion, the next big opportunity. Now those opportunities are

Launched upon Life by God's Word

past; but something more important lies ahead: to capitalise on the opportunities we have had, to make them come together into a true service that can be offered to God.

When we were younger, we knew ourselves to be spiritually underdetermined. We had lots of ideas, but we wore them like new, still uncomfortable clothes. They were possibilities, any one of which we could as easily think of realising as any other. Then the challenges of life took hold of us, and we began to appropriate them: some ideas fell away; others became part of the way we functioned, taking concrete form in the work we did, the priorities we set ourselves, the family that grew around us. But now we are determined, settled, of a piece with our ideas. We are what we are. Not at all! Paul tells us. The crucial determinations still lie before us. With age some of us have acquired a certain physical bulk the doctors tell us we must not try to carry around, but must lose. So it is with spiritual growth. Too much bulk, too much sense of what we are and where we have come, is not the real maturity. It has to be stripped off. We need to put ourselves back again in the place where anything is possible — not in order to dream about possibilities, for that is the final retreat from the world — but simply to discern the next challenge, the upward call that never allows us to settle back.

Facing Death

And the Lord answered Job out of the whirlwind. . . .   JOB 38:1

My mind has often dwelt on a poignant scene involving a colleague who died some years ago, John Norsworthy, who was our valued Cathedral Registrar officially and a good deal else to us unofficially. John loved the Lake District, where he used to go, ostensibly for refreshment but in fact to do what he did everywhere, which was make himself useful. A couple of weeks before he died a member of this congregation, happening to travel down the M6 and stopping off at the Tebay Services, caught sight of John's stocky figure standing and gazing at the hills in perfect stillness. She had the sensitivity to slip away unobtrusively and leave this last transaction uninterrupted. And since I heard that little story I have often wondered what kind of transaction it was, between a man of Christian faith confronting death and the unperturbed beauty of the mountain scenery. How do those two horizons intersect? That heavy-shouldered range of hills has seen me come, and now it sees me go. My going will not provoke even a cock of its head or a passing glance over its shoulder. Is it cruel that I must cease, and this go on? Or is it, in a curious way, comforting?

I was reminded of my question by the climax of the Book of Job, where the human sufferer, with all his burning sense of outrage, is presented with the vast pageant of nonhuman nature. The few verses that

22nd October 2000.

we read this morning are barely enough to get the flavour. One should read on and on and on, traversing with the author the dawning of the day, the springs of the ocean, the storehouses of snow and hail, the rain, the stars, the clouds, before coming to the animal kingdom: the lion, the mountain goat, the wild ass and the wild ox, the desert ostrich who provides the moment of comedy, the high-strung horse, the soaring hawk, and finally ferocious Behemoth and Leviathan, the hippopotamus and crocodile, our author turning to the Nile for the most exotic, spine-chilling members of his bestiary. All these have one thing in common: they go on their way with settled purpose and breathtaking grandeur, and without the slightest concern for our interests. They simply dwarf us.

That dwarfing, for the author of the Book of Job, is what the human sufferer needs. It is the only answer to the stream of complaint and reproach that he pours forth against God and the world. Job, who is all of us when we are suffering, is imprisoned in a contradiction. He sees the world as a forum where everyone should get their rights. He wants to hammer on the doors of the universe, like the woman in Jesus' parable, and force the authorities to do their job. The comforters, on the other hand, who are all of us when we are *not* suffering, find Job's state of mind to be inaccessible to reason. Their just perspectives, from which they can see the place of suffering in human affairs, are not open to him. How, our author wonders, can suffering dissolve the human point of view on the world into irreconcilable universes? What can bring the sufferer to reality? Nothing but liberation from the anthropocentric framework, the insistence on weighing the world on human scales, asking it human questions instead of taking it as it is.

Was that, then, the essence of the matter for our friend as he stood gazing out over the Cumbrian hills that day? "Little man, the ending of your life is no more than a moment in this great pageant! Be content to have observed it for a brief moment, and go your way!" We should not underestimate the comfort there may be in just that hard transaction. When I was younger, I used to be suspicious of the idea of coming to terms with death like that. Dylan Thomas told his dying father to "rage, rage against the dying of the light", and I confess I used to think that rather fine. But I don't any more. Humility and simple acceptance are not negligible virtues, and many have had just those to call on when their time has come. Yet the author of the Book of Job was a very subtle man, who liked to adopt different angles on the same events, and there was more than one light in which he wanted to study Job's final humiliation.

The Lord, he tells us, *answered Job out of the whirlwind.* The pageant of nature that ensues, sun, ocean, snow and hail and rain, stars and clouds, lion, goat, ass, ox and ostrich, mettlesome horse and soaring hawk, the ferocious bulk and jaws of Behemoth and Leviathan, all these are *what* God answered. But there is a reality more important than these: there is the *fact that* God answered. Which was what Job had been demanding all along. So the drama of the book, which from one point of view is the *overcoming* of Job, the breaking open of his enclosed perspective, is, from another point of view, the *vindication* of Job in his quest for personal accounting with God. *Gird up your loins,* says God, *like a man, and I shall question you!* It is by no means "like a man" to gird up his loins before God! To be put on the spot by the author of his nature! It is by no means what man's petty purchase on the universe would suggest! Here is a privilege granted neither to Behemoth nor to Leviathan. The hills which watch impassively the coming and the going of a thousand human generations have not exchanged a word with the one who put them there. Man may be dwarfed; man may need to know he is dwarfed. Yet man has been given a point of address. Man is spoken to. Man may hear a word more original and more final than the impassive silence of the natural universe.

And so it is that generations of Christian men and women, facing death, have known that they were to meet their maker and be judged. In that simple phrase, which sounds so flat to the ear, is wrapped up a deep mystery, a mystery far deeper than that of the universe. It is the mystery of God's engagement with us. He will not let us be, to return as clay to clay, but will summon us to gird up our loins and answer him. Much more may be said about the question that will be put to us and the answer we may give. We have heard in the Epistle and the Gospel of a high-priestly sacrifice and self-giving ransom. Yet we have grasped the heart of it if we have known that God has spoken to us and calls us to stand before him. In life, in death, there is exchange between God and man. God justifies himself to us; God justifies us to himself.

Launched upon Life by God's Word

*   *   *

You, Lord, give direction to every impulse: the striding of our feet, the glancing of our eyes, the darting of our affections, and the groping of our intelligence. Guard us from all that would sweep us off our course, and bring us to safe harbour in your promise.

Conclusion: No End to the Word

Proclaiming the kingdom of God and teaching about the
Lord Jesus Christ with complete boldness and unhindered.   ACTS 28:31

And that is the way St. Luke ends his account of the early church's mission in the Acts of the Apostles, which in its second half has become an account of Paul's mission. Those two striking expressions make a self-conscious final cadence: with complete boldness and unhindered. Greek rhetoric was well aware of the force of a negative prefix, and "unhindered" was certainly meant to be the final word. We can think of other possible conclusions that might have attracted Luke. Readers have always been struck by the emphatic statement earlier in this last chapter reporting the gospel's arrival at the heart of empire: *And so we came to Rome!* (28:14). That was a climax on which he might have ended. Or he might have ended, and very nearly did, with the decision to direct the Western mission towards Gentiles: *they will listen!* (28:28). And there were later events, of which Luke must surely have known, that could have provided strong endings: Paul's greatest sacrifice, his martyrdom; or the arrival in Rome of Peter, the other leading character in Acts. Each of these alternatives would have served a certain view of early history.

But Luke will not take his leave on any of these notes. His conclusion is that the proclamation and teaching do not conclude. The only ending to be made in church history, till Christ appears in judgment, is

16th July 2006.

that there is no end to the freedom of the word of God, which is what gives sense not only to church history, but to world history, too. And when today we have to bring an end to one episode in one person's life and ministry, what other point of rest could there be than the ongoing, restless freedom of God's word? It will be active through whatever ages remain, and it runs, as the Psalm says, swiftly. It clears aside all obstacles to its progress, obstacles within and obstacles without. Unfavourable circumstances and hostile institutions stand in its way; yet the proclamation and the teaching is unhindered. They are forced to step back, to concede it social space. In our own lifetimes we have seen just such a miracle take place in China. Under house arrest and with a Roman soldier at his side day and night, Paul turns his rented accommodation into a school, where God's deeds are daily announced, reflected on, celebrated. *Princes put pressure on me,* sang the ancient Psalm, *but to no effect; my heart stands in awe of thy words* (Ps. 119:161).

But the word of God does not attain its freedom simply by pushing aside external opposition. Religious *liberty* does not amount to religious *freedom.* Other hindrances that block its way may lie within. These, too, are cleared aside, allowing Paul to speak *with complete boldness.* "Boldness" is the essence of freedom; it is *parrhêsia,* open speech. And it is not constructed circumstantially from without; it is a disposition of mind. Not a gift of temperament, not an expression of special genius, not a peculiar stubbornness of character, but simply a matter of being possessed by the word, of having one's whole sense of things illumined by *its* sense.

It is not confined, therefore, to those who take the lead in speaking in public. Paul was not the only one to exercise boldness in Rome at that time. Had the believers and enquirers who were residents or visitors in the imperial city been of that stamp that defers too much to public correctness, they would never have beaten their path to Paul's little school in Trastevere, sat there day by day in his presence, listening, asking, discussing, right under the observant eyes of the authorities. *My heart stands in awe of thy words.* They had freedom of speech, too. *Take heed how you hear!* insisted Jesus (Mark 4:24). For hearing demands boldness. Everyone who has done anything, however humble, in the way of speaking God's word knows that everything depends on the way the listeners do their job. It is not uncommon, I find, to be approached after preaching by somebody who thanks one for saying this or that, when in fact one never did say this or that! Sometimes, to be sure, this or that was something better left unsaid; the hearer has failed to grasp or to articulate, and has seized on a triviality. But sometimes it is something that could and should have been said. It is the sermon God would have had the preacher deliver, if the preacher had been attentive enough. Communication of the word of God is always *tri-polar* communication, involving speaker, hearer, and the Spirit of God within both.

In pursuit of the connexion between boldness and hearing, let us make a brief diversion to a very different kind of preacher from Paul. The wonderfully told story of Balaam in the Book of Numbers tells how a professional soothsayer was converted into a real prophet, speaking the words of God. Balaam was a Moabite; as a religious figure he appears to have been a complete professional, the kind of person the King of Moab needed on his staff when facing the crisis of Israel's invasion. He knew that Balaam could speak with power; that was why he wanted him there. The miracle was that Balaam began to speak with freedom, too: to speak of God's promises and purposes for Israel and the world right before the face of the infuriated potentate. *God is not man that he should lie, or a son of man, that he should repent* (Num. 23:19). How Balaam acquired that freedom is the point of the story. It didn't come by having external hindrances removed. On the contrary, hindrances were piled up in front of him, one after another. As we read of how he was first approached, consulted God, and said No; then was approached again with a bigger fee, consulted God, and was told to make strict conditions; had the conditions accepted, set out, and then found his way blocked, and finally was told to press ahead after all, we can hardly help feeling a little indignant for this dutiful figure, who attempted to act in an orderly and responsible way but was so horribly messed about. Perhaps our minds may go to the negotiations that sometimes surround academic appointments! But it was all to achieve one thing: Balaam had to learn to listen, not to the King, not to his own professional judgment, but to the voice of YHWH himself. Balaam is famous for having had an angry altercation with his ass, which is a nice parable for what must happen to anyone who will become a mouthpiece for God. The ass represents all that Balaam has acquired of professional skill, judgment, and reputation; he has ridden to and fro about the world on this ass all his life. And now the ass has reached the point

Launched upon Life by God's Word

where it can go no further, where the road is blocked before it. Initially Balaam does not understand, and thinks he can drive the ass on to tackle this job as he has tackled so many before it. *Your way is perverse before me!* says the angel. The prophetic spirit can only go on alone, wholly dependent on the Spirit of God, independent of all else, responsive, attentive, disposable. Balaam will become the prophet he is to be when he becomes the man, as he describes himself, *who hears the words of God, falling down with his eyes uncovered.* Then he will be bold to speak, because he will have heard. *Faith comes through hearing,* said St. Paul (Rom. 10:17). If we are to attain the boldness of faith, we shall have to know that the words proclaimed *must* be heard, the words taught *must* be understood, let who will forbid it!

Proclaiming and teaching: that pair of verbs is a favourite with Luke. Proclamation and teaching are aspects of the same word; the lesson that is taught is no different from the message that is proclaimed. Yet we should not ignore that it has two aspects. The word of God contains not only a story of salvation — that "old, old story" that the mission hymn talked about — but an ongoing exposition and clarification. Faith receives, and faith seeks understanding. Deeper and deeper the word opens itself to us; deeper and deeper it penetrates us, shaping the life of the mind, refashioning every idea, motive, and purpose. *It destroys arguments and every proud obstacle to the knowledge of God, and takes every thought captive to obey Christ* (2 Cor. 10:5). A proclamation may be repeated over and over again, but a teaching must always be *pursued,* with interrogation, exploration, reconceptualisation. And perhaps this is represented by the role of a Canon Professor at Christ Church, that amphibious vehicle, or duplicitous construction, which converts from a pulpit to a chair and back again. Not two jobs, as I have often had to explain, but one job, in which two aspects of God's word are served together in their unity.

Paul's boldness had everything to do with the fact that for him the word of God was not only proclamation but teaching, not only an announcement rehearsed, repeated, and defended, but a wisdom that beckoned, a lamp to his feet and a light to his path, a key to the world, its history and its destiny. The word of God was the sweat of his brow, but it was also the life of his mind. Our juncture of history is rather like Paul's in one respect: it requires a Christian preacher to come to the defence of the life of the mind. As Universities daily conform themselves more closely to the school of wizardry in children's fiction, a repository of magic techniques to get startling effects, who else is left to care for how people, as individuals, think for themselves about the coherence of understanding, principle, and purpose that makes the difference between living in freedom and living in servitude? As the young flock in ever greater numbers to our Universities and colleges, who is there to talk to them seriously, and with all the resources of refined scholarly culture, about the meaning of their human existence, about how a vast quantity of scattered or organised information can be distilled into something worth a human being's while to be occupied with in his or her one and only venture at life? Of course, we shall be told that virtue cannot be taught, that the existential dimension of wisdom is something each person must discover for him or herself, not a topic for inclusion in a syllabus, to be "covered" in a tutorial. All of which is perfectly true. Yet wisdom can be present or absent as a goal and a horizon, before which everything covered in a syllabus can begin to assume its real importance. But this requires teachers who believe that learning is not simply perfecting a performance, but has to do with the terror and hope that is due to existence itself. It requires teachers who believe in the human reality of salvation and loss, who live out their academic roles as those who continually ask how they may be saved.

And what of the church, meanwhile? The language of salvation is its native language. The terror of loss and the hope of God's appearing are its native moods. The tale of God's wonderful deeds of redemption is its native text. *Blessed are those whom God chooses and brings near to dwell in his courts,* we sing (Ps. 65:4). Where is that blessing? *You shall lend to many nations but you shall not borrow,* it is promised (Deut. 28:12). Where is the wealth we have to lend? Do we find the church making good the lack in human wisdom that the narrowness of the schools has left? Do we hear its words make the world richer with their sound? In particular instances we can say it is so. The church has not wholly ceased to be the church. Yet the language, the mood, and the text seem all too often overwhelmed. And what is it that overwhelms them? Fear of the intellectual labour that the service of the word demands. When I say "intellectual", I do not mean, of course, that the church's ministry is, or ought to be, the preserve of scholars. God did not create most of the

Launched upon Life by God's Word

human race without intellectual powers sufficient for his service. It will be enough if we give ourselves wholeheartedly to the service we have been given.

"Something we were withholding made us weak", was Robert Frost's judgment on the early North American colonists. And the same may be said about the church. Something we are withholding makes us weak, withholding from the service of the word. It is not that we won't speak. Loud and repeated eructations are, today as always, not uncharacteristic of the church. But we won't devote the labour to speaking coherently, consistently, and faithfully. Have we really come to grips with the fact that the incarnate God came among us as a preacher, devoted his life to the spreading of a word, and summoned us to be his pupils? The life of the church — its fellowship, its sacraments, its order — are simply outworkings of discipleship. Are we held back from the discourse of God's grace, God's wisdom, and God's law because we lack *all boldness?*

The Canon Professor has the privilege of moving between the two spheres, University and church, as one whose task is to hold those spheres together, to ensure that the church shall have something of the school about it and the school something of the church. Preaching and teaching, then, the Canon Professor cannot be other than bold. He or she may abuse the right of boldness, as anyone may, by speaking out of turn or by assuming a bravado not supported by the labour on the word of God that has gone into it. He or she may sometimes overstay his welcome, not by insisting on things of first importance but by indulging a prosy taste for things of second importance. If this Canon Professor has offended in these respects, as surely from time to time he has, he asks for forgiveness. But for one thing he must be unapologetic. There is a word to be spoken: a descriptive word that tells us of God's presence in the world; a commanding word that directs us to the good works prepared for us; a reconciling word that attunes us to our situation; a word of judgment that displays what is right; a reasonable word, illuminating the logic of our situation and its demands; a word of salvation that delivers us from self-destruction. It is God who speaks this word when others speak it, God who will continue to speak it so long as history itself persists. And if the Canon Professors were to be silent, the very stones would cry out.

*   *   *

Turning, then, to the Lord our God, Father Son and Holy Spirit, we bless his name, uncreated, immortal, all-powerful, sovereign over history and the life of humankind; praying that what is lacking he will supply, what is amiss he will correct, and what is cold he will inflame with the ardour of his undying love, now and always.